IMAGES
of America

THEATRES OF
PORTLAND

Portland, Oregon, once had its own "Great White Way," a street known as Seventh Avenue until 1913. At that time, with the sprouting of large vaudeville houses, someday to become movie palaces, the street was renamed Broadway. This is how it looked about 1930. Today vaudeville has come and gone. The golden age of the movie palace has come and gone. But it is still called Broadway in honor of a way of life that captured all, whether it be the image of the moving pictures or the spectacle of Hollywood glamour delivered to our doorsteps. Portland still has a large number of former theatre structures outside of the city center to visit and study. Thanks to images of what once was, we can still fill in the gaps to take us on a road down Portland's collection of movie houses. (Courtesy Gary Lacher.)

ON THE COVER: The one-week-old Oriental Theatre represented the pinnacle of movie house evolution to the people of Portland, Oregon. Opening December 31, 1927, the 2,040-seat Oriental stood in the middle of the block of Southeast Grand Avenue, between Morrison and Belmont Streets. It was built during a brief four-year construction period when faraway lands were a popular theme. (Courtesy Oregon Historical Society Research Library OrHi 55023.)

IMAGES
of America

THEATRES OF PORTLAND

Gary Lacher and Steve Stone

ARCADIA
PUBLISHING

Published by Arcadia Publishing
Charleston SC, Chicago IL, Portsmouth NH, San Francisco CA

Printed in the United States of America

Library of Congress Control Number: 2009920423

For all general information contact Arcadia Publishing at:
Telephone 843-853-2070
Fax 843-853-0044
E-mail sales@arcadiapublishing.com
For customer service and orders:
Toll-Free 1-888-313-2665

Visit us on the Internet at www.arcadiapublishing.com

CONTENTS

Acknowledgments   6

Introduction   7

1.   Entering the Palace Doors   9

2.   Not as Dressed Up   71

3.   Lost in the Neighborhoods   87

4.   The Survivors   99

5.   Some Final Scenes   117

Index   127

ACKNOWLEDGMENTS

Thanks to Maryann Campbell, director of the vast Oregon Historical Society (OHS) Research Library; Lucy Berkley and Evan Schneider, OHS photo lab production assistance; James D. Fox, head of Special Collections and University Archives, University of Oregon Libraries; Richard Beer of the Hollywood Theatre/Film Venture Oregon; Tim Hills, for the McMenamins' contributions; Brian Johnson, City of Portland archives; and Bob MacNeur, for pipe organ knowledge.

Thanks to Thomas Robinson, Peter Corvallis, and Alex Bendl for unique image contributions; Mike Mathews for endless exploring and photography of theatre buildings; Dick Prather for pioneering exhaustive databases and his projectionists' experience; Reynolds Wulf, Inc., and Sam Hull, for technical assembly skills assistance; and Dick Thompson and many others for advice, patience, and encouragement from their experiences.

Also acknowledgments go to the numerous people and organizations that preceded this project for years, without which the momentum would not have started: Bob Rothschild, Laura Parker, the Architectural Heritage Center, Mike Clark, Dick Groat, Joe Beeler, and the staffs and management of Portland movie houses over the years, and sadly, those who could not wait long enough to enjoy it: Gary Fine, Bill Hayes, and Emily DeLano.

Personal thanks from Steve Stone to Chuck Nakvasil, whose Crest Theatre started so much. Personal thanks from Gary Lacher to his family and friends who have shared, supported, and endured his movie passion.

INTRODUCTION

One of the fondest pleasures we have are memories of going to the movies. Not only do we remember the film we saw but also who we went with and perhaps where we sat in the audience. Included in those highlights would be the theatre we saw those movies in. Whether it was a Saturday kids' matinee, a Friday evening date, or a special family event, theatres themselves encompassed the movie-going experience.

Portland, Oregon, parallels the history of the movie industry. Beginning with novelty showings in transition from vaudeville houses at the dawn of the 20th century, to the nickelodeon period in the early 1900s, movie houses grew rapidly. In fact, Portland had as many as 72 theatres exclusively for films by 1915. Although theatre growth reflected many other American towns and cities of the time, Portland provided a special refuge for those rainy evenings. The city has actually had more theatre seats per capita than any other city in the country, a notable statistic. But the biggest and best was yet to come. The 1920s began the era of larger palatial theatres, in both downtown and some neighborhoods, designed by local architects. The experience of going to see films was greatly enhanced by large pipe organs and even stage shows in the larger theatres.

The introduction of sound introduced a new advance by 1928. Like most other cities, Portland theatres went through a great state of flux during the Depression of the early 1930s, with new ownerships and management, but audiences remained loyal in a period of reasonable and inexpensive entertainment. During World War II, Portland provided constant movie programs for shipyard workers in split shifts, around the clock. This was a reflection of movie going at its height, even for a few years after the war.

By the early 1950s, theatres were met with new challenges, particularly television, and had to meet with new technology, bigger screens, and better sound. Portland theatres installed CinemaScope, stereophonic sound, and, yes, even ran 3-D for a brief period. But the smaller theatres were unable to equip their buildings with equipment or compete with television and subsequently went dark. At this point, the old palaces were becoming far too expensive to maintain. They were cavernous, gloomy and not appealing to a modern audience, and many of them fell by the wayside.

But new ideas came on the scene, and new deluxe or remodeled theatres began appearing. The Fox evolved out of the Mayfair, complete with the newest CinemaScope and stereo sound. New achievements such as Cinerama were installed in the large Hollywood neighborhood theatre. One of the few original 70-mm road show presentations of *Oklahoma* was shown at J. J. Parker's Broadway. Many patrons enjoyed this immensely, and movies, as well as the theatres, could outshine the television experience.

Sadly, by the early 1970s, many small neighborhood and downtown theatres became distinctive in showing adult films, and it is only with this dubious credit that they survived at all.

Meanwhile, new and large neighborhood theatres began appearing in the outer areas of Portland, such as the Eastgate and the Westgate in nearby Beaverton, supplementing the older downtown palaces that still existed or had been torn down. This was the deluxe style of the 1970s. The 1980s introduced the new mall-oriented theatre with eventual stadium seating, digital sound, and other enticements. Ironically some of those have already disappeared.

Meanwhile, theatres had to keep reinventing themselves. Again Portland led the way for the film community by establishing a new form of film entertainment: the brew-pub theatre, restored out of older historic buildings, school auditoriums, and lodge halls. This was now an era where people could share a film with an audience and a pizza in a "living room" atmosphere.

By the new millennium, a new dynamic diversity in the arts community, as well as traditional movie-going habits, continues the film experience. Although technical film presentations have changed dramatically and theatres are somewhat different in style and atmosphere, one cannot deny the experience of whom you were with and where you were when you went to the movies in Portland.

City directories show a Palace Theatre from 1909 through 1915 on Southwest First Avenue, between Madison and Main Streets. This is the doorman at the Palace, awaiting his duty to greet and open the door for patrons. The picture of the day is 1913's *Saved by Airship*. The theatre itself was not really a palace but rather a typical nickelodeon. The People's Amusement Company, in a 25-foot-wide, 100-foot-deep former storefront in a three-story building, operated it. But it was a retreat for people to escape into another world—a world not only of celluloid, but a world of developing architecture that people would attach themselves to. Portland, Oregon, just as the rest of the country, has been home to many such places. So let's prepare to enter the Palace doors. (Courtesy Dick Prather.)

One

ENTERING THE

PALACE DOORS

The most impressive examples of Portland movie theatres, as in the case of most other American cities, are images of the downtown palaces. Because of early stage and vaudeville houses, people became used to the best in showmanship and entertainment. When films began taking on their own programming, theatre owners wanted to impress their audiences with the best in atmosphere, and it was not long before auditoriums were built to provide at least 1,000 seats for single-screen entertainment. People were delighted and impressed with large palatial auditoriums that would let them escape from their daily routines and into another world of luxury and opulence, if only for a few hours.

Included with first-run feature films and surroundings, theatres also provided stage shows and even had their own fully staffed orchestras. It was not unusual to watch a complete stage presentation of musical and novelty acts before the films even started. Even theatres, which did not have an orchestra, at least had a giant pipe organ that supplemented the many sound effects and music that accompanied the films. Silent films were never shown silent. In fact, the sound of a live orchestra or pipe organ was just as impressive as the latest digital technology today. Sensing the live orchestra and performers below the screen was certainly a wonderful accompaniment to the film. When sound began arriving in Portland in 1927, audiences accepted the transition to a certain extent, but the live music was missed by many as the orchestras and stage shows disappeared.

Stage theatres began conforming to stricter safety codes in 1910. The new Heilig show house opened July 22, 1910, at Southwest Seventh Avenue (now Broadway) and Taylor Street. Gas-illuminated torches ring the top edge of the building. Besides Heilig's stock players, other stage and vaudeville acts would lease the building seasonally. E. W. Houghton was the lead architect. (Courtesy OHS OrHi 17527.)

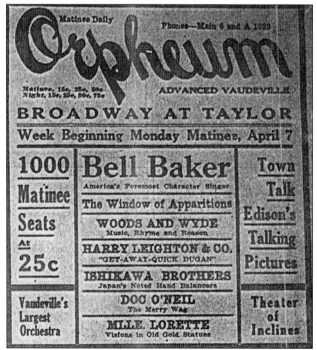

The show house from the very beginning had provisions for exhibiting moving pictures. Here, during the spring of 1913, the Orpheum vaudeville circuit is appearing at the Heilig. Note Edison's very early "talking" pictures are part of the program. This was accomplished with a synchronized phonograph system near the stage. (Courtesy Steve Stone.)

The 1,500-seat Heilig auditorium had box seats, which were typical for all of Portland's live and vaudeville houses. It had almost an opera house look throughout. Not many Portland theatres, live or motion picture, were equipped with an upper, second balcony, or gallery. Stage facilities were unequaled west of the Mississippi at the 1910 opening. (Courtesy OHS OrHi 68417.)

The gallery had been a segregated affair, accessible via a separate, unmarked side entrance to the five-story stairwell leading to a very plain ticket window at the top. Straw-stuffed benches, rather than orchestra seating, were offered for 10¢ cheaper than the main floor or first balcony admission. This area became sealed off in 1929 but was still intact, as this 1997 view shows. (Courtesy OHS bb004514.)

In 1929, the Paramount-Publix chain leased the theatre and made many renovations, including a very splashy marquee. The house became a double-feature movies and vaudeville venue for the chain. Talking equipment was installed. But the Depression was just starting, and Paramount would pull out after only two years of operating. (Courtesy Alex Blendl.)

After other operators took brief turns at experimenting with movies and stage shows, it came under the operation of the now-established J. J. Parker chain of regional movie houses. The marquee was re-lettered Mayfair and the interior redecorated thoroughly. Economy double features became the mainstay, punctuated with regular road show stage events. (Courtesy OHS OrHi 25794.)

Very typical of the downtown palaces was the "island" box office, such as the one at the Mayfair. The cashier on duty would be the attractive focal point to consummate the purchase of tickets. Until the 1960s, other service staff (except management) normally could not work, or even enter, the box office. All daily receipts were counted in double custody and deposited in a drop-safe. (Courtesy OHS OrHi 25840.)

Stepping inside, there was the lobby entrance, with recessed dome and chandelier. The stairs in the background lead to a set of basement lounges, typical of most of the vaudeville houses. Another set was located on the mezzanine level and a separate pair, five floors up, for patrons of the galleries. Other lobby amenities, not pictured, of this 1910-era, were a checkroom for coats and a gentlemen's smoke stand. (Courtesy OHS OrHi 25841.)

Little of the Heilig auditorium was altered. Here is a view of the proscenium. There was an optical-effect machine in the projection booth that could create a pattern of drifting clouds on the ceiling above the painted skyline. During the movie presentation era, the box seats were not used. (Courtesy OHS OrHi 25842.)

A feature rather novel at the time of original 1910 construction was the use of ramps, rather than stairways, to gain access from the main floor to the first balcony. This was the handiwork of one of the up-and-coming associate architects, Benjamin Priteca. Priteca would soon work with the Alexander Pantages circuit and be its main designer for over a decade. (Courtesy OHS OrHi 25843.)

The management offices remained little changed over the entire 80-year life of the theatre. It demonstrates that operation of theatres was once a very structured, and staffed, business affair. But by the 1980s, the rooms would only be frequented by staff reporting the cash receipts and changing clothes. (Courtesy OHS OrHi 25792.)

In this view, the larger, 1929 projection booth installation can just be seen in the dark former gallery area. The original booth had been high at the very back wall of the gallery behind the booth shown here. At the rear of the lower balcony, on the left, is still evidence of Calvin Heilig's private viewing box from his apartment. (Courtesy OHS OrHi 25838.)

The Mayfair closed in October 1953 for nine months of renovations to create the newest style of Fox West Coast Theatre. Part of a national goal, it would soon be a part of their brand-new CinemaScope line of movie houses. Their flowing underwater design was known as "Skouras-izing," named after Charles P. Skouras, head of Fox West Coast Theatres. (Courtesy Steve Stone Collection.)

As the exterior conversion neared completion, a crane lifts the last of three segments comprising the massive vertical sign. When the theatre was demolished some 43 years later, the sign was again a spectacle for onlookers when the building facade was toppled all at once early one Sunday morning onto Southwest Broadway. Dougan and Heims was the Portland architectural firm for the conversion. (Courtesy Steve Stone Collection.)

Gold-leaf stenciling is shown as it was being applied on ceiling surfaces of the lobby and outside entry. It also was used extensively on walls of the lobby, staircases, and mezzanine lounge. It just goes to show that in this era of movie house construction, no expense was spared to get the details. (Courtesy Steve Stone Collection.)

As high as the new ceiling was for the new Fox, it was suspended from the even higher original Heilig ceiling by a network of cables. The original proscenium, stage, and box seats were completely removed, but the majority of the upper balcony floor remained, as well as the gallery box office and restrooms. (Courtesy Steve Stone Collection.)

Twentieth Century–Fox chartered an airliner, calling it the "CinemaScope Special," and filled it with stars from Hollywood to promote the opening. Stars included Van Heflin, Rita Moreno, Johnnie Ray, Mary Murphy, Edward Arnold, Mamie Van Doren, and Rex Allen. (Courtesy Steve Stone Collection.)

The public was on hand to greet the 60-passenger flight, as well as state and city officials. Here the motorcade is shown ready to leave the Portland International Airport, with motorcycle escorts, for the 6-mile trip to downtown's Benson Hotel. (Courtesy Steve Stone Collection.)

The souvenir program cover commemorating the Thursday, August 12, 1954, opening of the "Million Dollar" Fox Theatre was given to all 1,536 invited guests. Special parking passes to area garages were also issued, as well as the reserved seat tickets for the premiere of the CinemaScope picture, *Broken Lance*. (Courtesy Steve Stone Collection.)

This ice sculpture, re-creating the Fox facade and vertical sign, was created for dignitaries and invited dinner guests at the Benson Hotel. After the banquet, a motorcade took dignitaries and stars to the Fox Theatre, five blocks away. (Courtesy Steve Stone Collection.)

Bleachers for 2,000 spectators were placed across Broadway from the theatre to view the opening festivities. Local radio and television celebrities were on hand, followed by Portland's Rose Festival Queen of 1954 and her festival court. A stage had been assembled in front of the box office for the events. At 8:00 p.m., the motorcade arrived from the Benson Hotel. (Courtesy Steve Stone Collection.)

A view of the filled auditorium of invited guests reveals a sea of white tuxedos and best dress of those attending such an important event. Lavish openings would never be the same after this. All had also been given special parking stickers to designated area garages. (Courtesy Steve Stone Collection.)

Even though the Fox ceiling was suspended about 20 feet beneath that of the former Mayfair, it still maintained an impressive height above the auditorium. Behind the curtains was the huge CinemaScope screen, measuring 32 by 63 feet. At the 1954 opening, it was promoted as the second largest screen in the country, being only 2 feet smaller than that of the Roxy in New York City. (Courtesy Steve Stone Collection.)

A view of the freshly finished south auditorium wall, with its theme of an undersea decor, is pictured here. This is the final result after slight revisions were made to the initial plastering. Officials of the theatre chain (National Theatres and Evergreen Theatres) had not been satisfied with the initial effort. Auditorium illumination came from blue and white neon in the cove ringing the ceiling. (Courtesy Steve Stone Collection.)

The gold-leaf stencil work flows outward over the box office. This photograph shows carpeting that had to be installed within weeks after opening. The original rubber matting beneath contained a pattern of small holes that unintentionally captured high heels. (Courtesy Steve Stone Collection.)

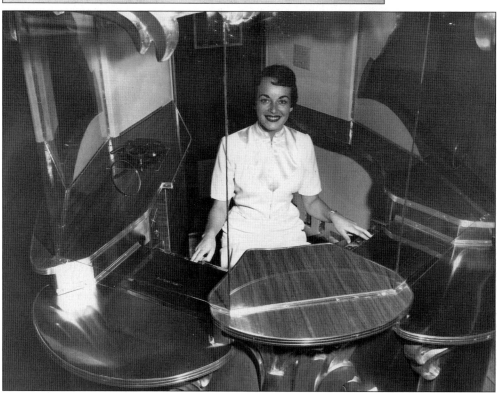

The box office was crafted by a California company, shipped to Portland, and assembled. Constructed of stainless steel skirting and molded plaster scrollwork, it had two cashier windows. There were two ticket machines initially, but there was insufficient room for two cashiers unless they stood. The machine on the left was soon removed. (Courtesy Steve Stone Collection.)

The public gets its first look at the new Fox Theatre at 11:00 a.m. the next day, Friday, August 13, 1954. The feature was *Broken Lance* with Spencer Tracy. During the early weeks and months, patrons would hear a specially recorded "welcome to your new Fox Theatre" announcement in the auditorium before the show would start. (Courtesy Steve Stone Collection.)

The huge concession counter was another sign of the spacious opulence of the Fox. It would not be surpassed in size until the evolution of the multiplex cinema some 15 years away. But there was something that was too much. Some patrons and staff were so overwhelmed with seeing themselves in so many surfaces that adhesive wall covering was applied to some of the mirrors. (Courtesy Steve Stone Collection.)

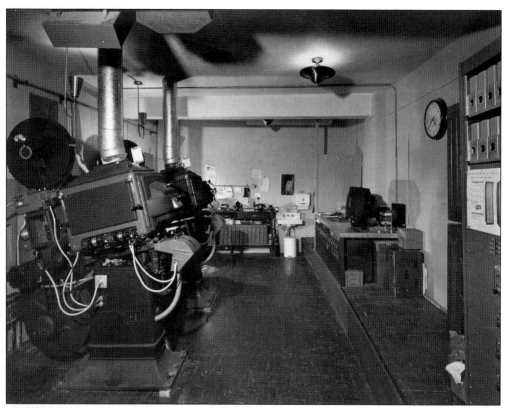

The projection booth was very spacious looking. That was somewhat unintentional, as original plans allowed for a third projector that was never installed. The house was Portland's first constructed for the new 35-mm CinemaScope system. A few other theatres had converted in previous months. Later 70-mm equipment would be installed. (Courtesy Steve Stone Collection.)

Reminiscent of a scene from *Cinema Paradiso*, a publicist seems to have staged this shot of a pesky, youthful staff member and a Fox projectionist. The machine operator is threading the Ampex four-track magnetic sound head of the equipment, which presented sound from three front channels and one channel for the surround speakers. The throw to the massive screen was 122 feet. (Courtesy Steve Stone Collection.)

From the end of World War II until the mid-1950s, Fox Theatres "Skouras-ied" about 200 houses nationwide. The only other such retrofit in the state occurred in Eugene. This massive finished sign was the largest and brightest (75,000 watts) ever for any Portland movie house. The Fox vertical lettering was white neon within a red circle. The filigree was sea green with gold accent links. Many Portlanders still recollect watching *The Sound of Music* playing here for over two years. That was a record run for any downtown movie house. The Fox also was equipped with closed-circuit television projection that in later years would address the city's normally sold-out status of Trailblazer basketball games. Regularly scheduled movies ceased in September 1990. It was rented out for only a few more times for special events and then was demolished in 1997. Currently the 27-story Fox Tower occupies the whole block, including a 10-screen cinema inside. (Courtesy Steve Stone Collection.)

The second of Portland's palaces also started as a stage venue—the 1,200-seat Baker. Pictured here near its opening on September 17, 1910, at Southwest Morrison Street and Eleventh Avenue. It was modified from the shell of a former livery stable. It was constructed as home for the Baker Players, operated by well-known George Baker, a prolific Portland showman and later mayor. Inferior acoustics caused it to close almost immediately for two months of redesign. (Courtesy OHS bb004510.)

This theatre was equipped to show films as schedule filler. Other stage names were Dufwin (as shown here in 1932), Alcazar, Music Box, and El Capitan; it changed to the Playhouse in 1932, running mainly moving pictures thereafter. Closing in June 1950, it was used for church services and a few stage events, closing for good in October 1953. Demolition was in 1954. (Courtesy OHS bb004500.)

The Majestic Theatre was Portland's first "palace" constructed for motion picture presentation. At 1,100 seats, it broke the arbitrary 1,000-seat border defining "palace." Opening June 10, 1911, it was at the northeast corner of Southwest Park Avenue and Washington Street. In the background of this *c.* 1917 image is the 1904 stage theatre, the Star, which had been billing "Synchroscope films" as early as 1908. (Courtesy University of Oregon Libraries.)

In 1929, owners sold to J. J. Parker Theatres, and renovations began to transform it to the United Artists Theatre, for which it is most known. The firm of Bennes and Herzog, responsible for crafting the Hollywood Theatre three years earlier, was the designer. Second-floor offices were transformed into a 40-by-100-foot lounge. (Courtesy OHS OrHi 26673.)

The interior also underwent exhaustive refitting, with this new proscenium and new stage. Mayor George Baker spoke at the rededication ceremonies on September 29, 1928. He spoke of the early days of theatre in Portland, having been personally involved for two decades himself in the industry. He also spoke of the early experiences of J. J. Parker, also a pioneer showman. (Courtesy OHS OrHi 26308.)

By the 1950s, most of the movie trade had shifted away from this first street of theatre concentration to Broadway. Once surrounded by at least five other such structures in a one-block radius, the Majestic closed in 1955 and was torn down in 1957 to make way for construction of the Bank of California Tower. (Courtesy OHS OrHi 68410.)

Five months after the Majestic came the People's Theatre, named after the People's Amusement Company that had pioneered Portland's earliest organized chain of nickelodeons. This was the company's largest, with seating for 1,095 patrons. The theatre opened November 1, 1911. Initially it faced West Park Avenue, which is now Ninth Street, near the corner of Alder Street. Newcomb Engineering designed the structure. (Courtesy Steve Stone Collection.)

Primarily of concrete construction, the People's Theatre did have a brick-veneer facade. The concrete balcony was poured in a record one-day event. This is a later view after being converted to the Alder Theatre. Above the street is one of several popular signs decorating city streets during the 1920s and 1930s in front of theatres. Most were about 45 feet long and weighed 2,000 pounds. (Courtesy Mike Mathews.)

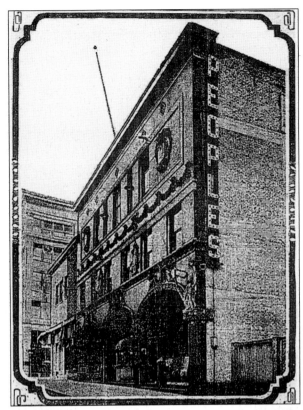

In 1929, the firm of Bennes and Herzog, working for the J. J. Parker Theatres chain, spent over $100,000 to renovate the house into the Alder Theatre. The entrance was moved up to the corner at Alder, for which it assumed the new identity. Here, like in the case of the United Artists, second-floor offices were altered to become an even larger lounge affair. (Courtesy OHS OrHi 68401.)

Steel girders replaced the previous five balcony support posts below. Seating was increased by about 100, along with a completely new projection booth. But the Depression was taking hold, and the theatre changed hands a year later to become a new location for the Music Box. In 1952, the house closed, eventually becoming the surface parking lot there today. (Courtesy OHS OrHi 68408.)

The Pantages vaudeville circuit moved into this spacious, "fire-proof," 1,400-seat structure on April 3, 1912. Located on the northwest corner of Seventh Avenue (now Broadway) and Alder Street, it cost $225,000 to erect. Emil Schact was the architect, but a later major renovation came under the helm of Benjamin Priteca. Short films were always billed at the bottom of the program. (Courtesy OHS bb004479.)

For its final period, November 1926 until the end of April 1928, it became a true movie house with talking equipment. It was the first of a series of six bearing the name Music Box in Portland for John Hamrick Theatres. After closing, the building was demolished to make room for Fred Meyer's Alderway Building. (Courtesy OHS OrHi 68385.)

Sullivan and Considine vaudeville circuit was the next on the Portland scene with their Empress Theatre at Seventh and Yamhill Street. Opening March 3, 1913, it originally seated 2,000, including balcony and box seating. Now with the street taking on the look of the "great white way," 10 days later, Seventh was renamed Broadway. By 1916, the theatre was the Hippodrome under the Leow's circuit. (Courtesy University of Oregon Libraries.)

In September 1926, Pantages took over, and Benjamin Priteca extensively redecorated the interior. But in September 1929, real change came when it became the R.K.O. Orpheum as well as a movie house. Pantages would return in a last attempt to resurrect his vaudeville chain for one brief year in the fall of 1933, when this picture was taken. (Courtesy OHS OrHi 11950.)

By October 1934, the Orpheum name was back, with the popular blend of double feature movies and several acts of vaudeville. While the caliber of stage stars and number of acts declined, it was still offered until March 1941. Minor, second-rate vaudeville would continue in the smaller houses for a number of years. (Courtesy Steve Stone Collection.)

The landmark vertical sign, originally constructed in 1926, was re-lettered Orpheum in 1929, then changed briefly back to Pantages, and then to Orpheum again in 1934. The 1,500-pound sign was 60 feet in height and 6 feet wide. Offices on the top three floors were rentals— one even being the Portland branch for the United Nations. KXL radio once had studios on the top floor. (Courtesy Steve Stone Collection.)

The Orpheum proscenium and stage are seen here as they looked about 1930. Lee De Camp was the original architect. In preparation to designing the theatre, he went to Salt Lake City to study the acoustics of the Mormon Tabernacle. His efforts produced an auditorium bearing superior results. (Courtesy Steve Stone Collection.)

In the 1930s, beneath the sidewalks surrounding the Orpheum, there existed a maze of narrow halls and rooms that was decorated for use by an extensive miniature golf operation. Note the exotic outdoor foliage depicted on the walls. (Photograph by Steve Stone.)

One of the Orpheum's dressing rooms beneath the stage is pictured here. In the 1960s and 1970s, they were mostly occupied by various groups of the service staff. This is a view of the doorman's room. One can only wonder what the walls would say, as many major vaudeville troupers played the Orpheum—Bob Hope, Eddie Cantor, George Burns, all of them. (Photograph by Steve Stone.)

The theatre stagehands of the season of 1918–1919 painted this name roster at one of the rigging platforms above the stage. One name, Moyer, stands out, though it is probably not part of another Moyer family that moved to Portland in 1919 and later started a chain of movie houses that eventually became Oregon's largest. (Photograph by Steve Stone.)

Although this is a 1953 view, taken after wall drapery had been installed, part of the classic 1926 star-shaped Pantages dome is still visible. It was a creation by Benjamin Marcus Priteca, a major theatre architect for the Pantages chain, who had gotten his start in Portland in 1910 working on the Heilig. Soon after he completed this work, he became a lead architect for Warner's Theaters. (Courtesy Steve Stone Collection.)

A design feature that was novel at the time was the "no post construction" of the balcony. This was the result of a 67-ton, 90-foot-long support girder. That same girder would cause a huge delay during the building's demolition in 1976. Seating was 1,750 at the time of this photograph in 1953. (Courtesy Steve Stone Collection.)

The Orpheum mezzanine lounge could accommodate as many as 200 persons awaiting performances. Large windows overlooked Broadway. Along with ample furnishings, the carpeting was of such quality that in the mid-1970s much of it was sold and removed to completely re-carpet the Film Fair Theatre in nearby Beaverton. (Courtesy Steve Stone Collection.)

Promotion of new movies was once a regular, every week process. Here is staff dressed in "sleep wear," along with two like-garbed mannequins, promoting 1955's *The Pajama Game*. Until the Orpheum's closure in 1976, there was a property room still containing these and many other usable props, including a small World War II bomb! (Courtesy Steve Stone Collection.)

This and the following two photographs chronicle the evolution of concession stands, at the Orpheum as well as of the industry. This *c.* 1930 view shows just a small counter. Often these were dominated by smokers' supplies. Sometimes finger foods, such as peanuts, were available but was more often pitched by walking aisle attendants during intermissions. (Courtesy Steve Stone Collection.)

This is the Orpheum snack bar, likely in the late 1940s. Now available are candy, drinks, and very importantly, popcorn. Note the tailored neon work displayed overhead. Refreshment counters by the 1940s had become as attractive and well lit as the exteriors. All of this was more to address the "creature comforts" of an evening out, but not as sophisticated as in the vaudeville era. (Courtesy Steve Stone Collection.)

The final Orpheum snack bar, seen in this 1952 view, is starting to take on the look of grocery store displays. Now the emphasis was not so much to pamper the patron but to hone the ability to keep ahead of the increased costs in all other areas of the theatre operation, now seeing annual declines in attendance. (Courtesy Steve Stone Collection.)

The grand staircase in the lobby was punctuated on its climb by several landings and turns, split with a banister down the middle. During the heyday of busy Disney performances, the stairway at intermissions resembled more a lava flow of endless kids. (Courtesy Steve Stone Collection.)

The projection booth, like most, was at the rear of the balcony. But the balcony, having been constructed for vaudeville crowds of 1913, was very steep. That resulted in the projectors being tilted down as seen here. That made for little clearance of both the feed and take-up reels on the projectors. Also, the screen on the stage had to be slightly tilted to prevent picture distortion. (Photograph by Steve Stone.)

In May 1976, as furnishings of the Orpheum were being sold and removed, original backdrops long contained in the fly-loft were dropped, and removed, one at a time. It is not known if they were salvaged or destroyed. This moment was caught only by accident. A Nordstrom's department store now occupies this entire block. (Photograph by Steve Stone.)

The Columbia Theatre opened in June 1913 on Southwest Sixth Avenue, between Stark and Washington Streets. At 1,100 seats, it became Portland's third such movie palace. The front of the building was faced with terra-cotta and white brick and outlined with 2,500 10-watt electric lights. Herbert L. Camp and Andrew Lowe DuPuy were noted as designers. (Courtesy OHS OrHi 17503.)

Columbia Theatre patrons are seen here preparing to attend a showing of Cecil B. DeMille's *The Road to Yesterday* in 1925. In 1935, the theatre became the Downtown, offering mostly economy sub-run and occasional revival films. Another attraction was the "Magic Drinking Fountains," activated when approached. (Courtesy OHS bb004476.)

In 1947, the entire facade was made over with this streamlined look, and the name became the Century. The interior, however, was changed little. On another note, the site previously was a small nickelodeon, from about 1909 until the Columbia was constructed. Sixth Avenue had seen a number of small such houses in the early years, including one of the pioneering Hale's Tours franchises. (Courtesy OHS CN007264.)

By 1952, the Century had become Portland's last newsreel theatre. Portland had just received its first television station in September 1952, but several newsreel companies were still producing weekly releases. But in 1955, and after two more television stations, the 20th Century News Theatre closed on March 30. A five-story bank headquarters replaced it in 1957. (Courtesy Steve Stone.)

Portland's fourth picture palace, the National, opened November 1, 1914, at Southwest Stark Street and Park Avenue. The 1,500-seat, four-story concrete and steel building exterior was white, highlighted with ornamental plaster, and outlined with 2,000 electric lights. A roof garden was also sited atop the building. (Courtesy OHS OrHi 76511.)

The National had a full stage, but motion pictures were always the primary attraction. A playground with swings, a slide, sand pile, hobbyhorses, wagons, and dolls was also available for children. This is a 1923 promotion set up in an attached storefront for *The Ten Commandments*. The theatre changed owners and names often, becoming the Strand (1916), Rivoli (1920), Pix (1939), and back to Rivoli (1939). (Courtesy OHS bb004478.)

In October 1941, it became Portland's first Newsreel Theatre. While newsreels themselves had long been an added staple to movie programs, this introduction of a house policy came at the start of World War II, fitting well with the increased population of the war effort workforce that operated 24 hours a day. It had the pick of product from RKO, MGM, Paramount, and Fox Movietone. (Courtesy Steve Stone.)

Just seven months before television arrived in the city, it next became the very popular sub-run, double-feature house, the Roxy, early in 1952. It was closed and demolished in 1958. This also shows the relocated main entrance from Southwest Washington Street, carved through an adjoining building in 1922. Now O'Bryant Square, a city park, graces the site. (Courtesy OHS OrHi 91253.)

The 2,200-seat Liberty Theatre was originally commissioned as the Broadway but opened under the Orpheum name on November 14, 1914. It was Portland's fifth moving picture palace constructed but was also extensively outfitted for vaudeville. It was constructed on the former site of the Portland Library Association building at Southwest Broadway and Stark Street and cost $350,000. This shows it as it appeared in June 1927. (Courtesy OHS OrHi 47752.)

The lobby contained a 6-foot-high statue showering water into a 6-foot-wide goldfish pond. In 1916, it became the T&D Theatre, for the Turner and Dahnken Circuit, their only such foray into Portland. Also that year, the first installation of a Wurlitzer pipe organ in the city occurred here. Several months afterward, the theatre became the Broadway before the Liberty name was first implemented in 1917. (Courtesy OHS OrHi 68412.)

John Hamrick introduced Vitaphone as well as a new name, the Music Box, in 1928. But the name Liberty returned in 1932. All throughout the years, first-run films were the mainstay programming. Following major remodeling in 1938, it reopened Christmas Eve, touting an "Exquisite Lounge for the ladies, life-like screen, and many other new features." (Courtesy Steve Stone Collection.)

Included in the renovations was this brilliant, brand-new reader board, containing 403 interior 40-watt bulbs, 500 exterior 10-watt bulbs, extensive neon surround, and fluorescent tubing. The Liberty would remain open until the closure and demolition in January 1959. But there was later life for many of the fixtures, which will be described later. (Courtesy OHS OrHi 68412.)

The next of the downtown palaces would be the Broadway Theatre, on Southwest Broadway between Salmon and Main Streets, on a parcel of land measuring 100 by 200 feet. Prominent local architect A. E. Doyle designed the building in Italian Renaissance-style. It was of reinforced concrete construction, with a tile hip roof. It is shown here under construction May 3, 1926. (Courtesy OHS bb004498.)

In the days of August leading up to the opening, this was the view of progress. This would be Doyle's only Portland theatre, although he did design nearby Vancouver, Washington's Castle Theatre about the same time. Doyle has left more of an imprint on the Portland scene than any other. Sadly, he passed away at age 50 just a year and a half after the Broadway opened. (Courtesy OHS OrHi 72065.)

A 1925 sketch depicted a slightly different structure that at the time was being planned to be the 2,500-seat Hippodrome Theatre, operated by the Ackerman and Harris vaudeville circuit. When they dropped out, the proposed name was changed to the Broadway and seating dropped to 2,200. (Courtesy OHS OrHi 63156.)

Final preparations are underway for the evening's opening of the Broadway on August 27, 1926. Searchlights were positioned, ready to sweep the sky that night as a low-flying de Havilland airplane swooped overhead, dropping thousands of rosebuds on the crowds below. With all the excitement, it was tainted somewhat by the worldwide sorrow over the passing three days earlier of Rudolph Valentino. (Courtesy University of Oregon Libraries.)

Thousands of people took free streetcar rides downtown to participate in the spectacle of the opening of the "Million Dollar Playhouse." Those who could not attend listened to festivities carried on KGW radio's live 90-minute broadcast, a local first for the time. Speakers were also set outside the theatre. Police estimated the crowds that night at 60,000 around the theatre and another 40,000 up and down Southwest Broadway. (Courtesy Laura Parker.)

A photograph of the staff being assembled for the Broadway, taken in July 1927, reveals only a portion of those employed. Floyd Maxwell (far right) is director; Allan Cushman (far left) is staff assistant; those wearing caps are doormen; all others between are the maids and usherettes. Not shown are the cashiers, projectionists, janitors, secretaries, organists, 20-piece orchestra, and many others necessary in running the theatre. (Courtesy OHS OrHi 73013.)

In January 1932, this "peacock"-style marquee was added. The letters inside the peacock fan were individual, changeable plug-in neon blocks. At the same time, the giant neon script lettering was added to the side of the building. During World War II, an additional large "V" victory letter was constructed above, a sign of the patriotic support J. J. Parker Theatres carried out during those years. (Courtesy OHS bb004497.)

This September 1939 view from the same angle is even more spectacular by night, with the revelation of flashing lights and extensive neon use. By the 1970s, operators of the theatre had eliminated the regular changing of the neon block letters, opting just to spell out permanently "Broadway Tri-Cinema." (Courtesy OHS bb004492.)

This was the main-floor lobby. The entrance to the ladies' lounge is the doorway to the left. In the 1940s, a large concession counter would be placed against the wall on the right, at the head of two aisle doors. The ceiling pattern of rows of waves mimics the look of that in the auditorium, as well as rows of concrete canopies on the building's exterior. (Courtesy OHS bb004495.)

The "Million Dollar Playhouse" had all the amenities deserving of a first-class palace. This was the graceful stairway leading to the plush mezzanine lounge. A matching, but less used, stairway was at the opposite end of the foyer. When the theatre was divided into a separate screen in the 1970s, a 3-foot-high divider was installed in the middle all the way up to the mezzanine. (Courtesy OHS bb004491.)

This is what the foyer at the top of the grand staircase looked like in 1932. Theatre offices were on the right, as well as ramps leading to the balcony. To the left was the entrance to the large mezzanine lounge. In the 1970s, this foyer area featured a second concession counter. Jack Matlack, renowned local publicist, maintained his offices for decades here as well, promoting many premieres and events. (Courtesy OHS bb004494.)

This is the large, richly furnished mezzanine lounge. Years later, the area was converted to Portland's well-known Amato's Supper Club. In 1964, it was transformed into the 450-seat Off-Broadway Theatre, with separate box office and entrance on Southwest Salmon Street. Foreign and art films played until 1971, at which time it became accessible from the Broadway's main entrance and was programmed as a multiplex venue. (Courtesy OHS bb004493.)

A view of the theatre auditorium interior and west wall, from 1932, shows the orchestra pit below as well. The Broadway had a four-manual "Special" Wurlitzer pipe organ until 1955. At that time, it was relocated to the Oaks Amusement Park, where it continues to be used to this day in the roller rink. In 1971, the balcony was converted into a separate, third auditorium. (Courtesy OHS OrHi 68371.)

Architect Doyle commented at the opening, "In the design we have been prompted by the thought that a theatre is built for the public. Our objective is to secure crowds. From the beautiful design of the entrance we progress naturally to the interior. Comfort is paramount. Art in architecture as well as other things is determined by its lasting value as a thing of beauty." (Courtesy OHS OrHi 25851.)

The Broadway had 22 wrought-iron light fixtures. The six largest ones contained 150 light bulbs each. All of them had multiple lighting circuits, so any color or combination of colors red, blue, amber, or green could be controlled from the projection booth. (Courtesy OHS OrHi 32042.)

An early view of the Broadway stage, with the picture screen raised, exposes the full stage. By 1953, a larger, 42-foot-wide, 20-foot-high curved screen was installed, facilitating later installation of 70-mm projection equipment to show Todd-A-O and CinemaScope features. The year 1953 also saw the Broadway bring key 3-D films such as *House of Wax* to Portland audiences. (Courtesy OHS OrHi 25856.)

A view of the stage captures the control panel off to the side. All functions could be controlled from the projection booth as well, rather than using a stagehand backstage. The stage itself was adequate for the regular vaudeville of the first few years but not for major stage events. In the 1980s, the stage was converted to a small fourth screen for about 100 persons. (Courtesy OHS OrHi 25858.)

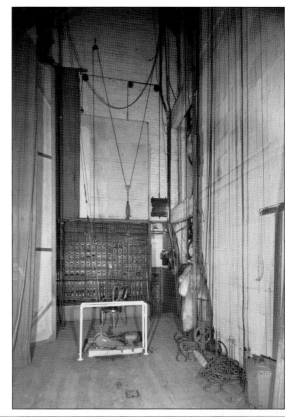

This is a view of one of the 10 dressing rooms backstage at the Broadway shortly before demolition. After the first few brief years of vaudeville, these rooms and the stage facilities received irregular use other than for storage. The theatre was closed and torn down in 1988 to make room for the current 24-story 1000 Broadway Building, with its four-screen cinema. (Courtesy OHS OrHi 25862.)

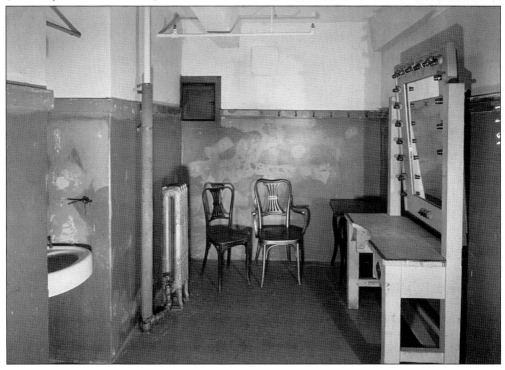

PROJECTION ROOM
BROADWAY THEATRE- PORTLAND, ORE.

ANGELUS
81138

The projection booth is seen here in 1941. The three original projectors are gone, but the bases remain. Replacement projectors are likely the result of 1932 theatre renovations and are early Simplex E-7s, with Brenkert Enarc carbon-arc lamp houses. Additionally, there was a Brenkert effects machine and two spotlights. The wall in the rear contains a full set of stage controls. (Courtesy University of Oregon Libraries.)

"The Magic Sign of a Wonderful Time" was the motto of the Broadway when it opened. And "wonderful" was an apt way to describe the impressive, 60-foot-high vertical sign. The 2,000-pound sign cost $4,500 in 1926 and was outfitted with 4,048 light bulbs. In 1929, that number was reduced to accommodate the introduction of neon tubing. (Courtesy OHS bb004499.)

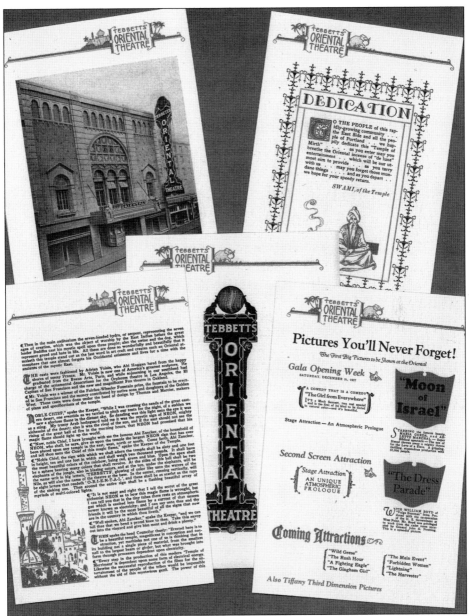

Beyond this souvenir program are the story and images of what most consider the finest movie palace ever to be constructed in Portland. Walter Eugene Tebbetts, established movie house operator, persuaded George Weatherly, a local ice cream magnate, to construct the largest house ever sited on the city's east side. It exceeded the 1,396-seat Bagdad Theatre that opened January 14, 1927, and the 1,496-seat Hollywood Theatre, which had opened July 17, 1926. Only the Portland Theatre in 1928 would handle more patrons. Originally, it had no name, being referred to as "Building for the Crystal Ice and Storage Company." The design theme followed a trend—faraway lands—embodied in other local show houses, such as the Granada, Venetian, Chaldean, Egyptian, and Bagdad theatres. The Oriental Theatre became the project name and would be connected to Portland's first skyscraper on the east side of the Willamette River being built by Weatherly. Lee Thomas and Albert Mercier were the project architects. (Courtesy Robertson, Hay, and Wallace.)

Ground was broken on March 21, 1927, for the 2,038-seat playhouse, with work progressing as shown here by August 30. The vastness of the interior is elusive to convey. Temporary 60-foot supports hold the frame for the roof in place, as concrete for the 75-foot-wide, 155-foot-long auditorium floor is being placed. I-beams are in place for construction of the balcony, itself over 100 feet long. (Courtesy Robertson, Hay, and Wallace.)

The nearly finished, prominent, 12-story Weatherly Building stands alongside the theatre on December 31, 1927. The Oriental awaits its grand opening later that evening. Cost of the combined project was in excess of $1.5 million. Ironically, this photograph was taken from atop one of several smaller movie houses in the area, the Crescent, being displaced. Even Tebbetts's first theatre, the Empire, seven blocks south, would be a casualty. (Courtesy Robertson, Hay, and Wallace.)

This second week of January 1928 photograph shows the new Oriental Theatre, offering up its second program, William Boyd in *Dress Parade*. Advertisements proclaimed "the only first run downtown east side playhouse." The Morrison Bridge crossing Portland's Willamette River to downtown was at the foot of Belmont, the street crossing Southeast Grand Avenue on the far side of the Weatherly Building next to the theatre. City planners had envisioned connecting two intersecting boulevards into Belmont close to this point, funneling all east-side traffic through the intersection leading downtown, where all other first-run movie houses were located. The fact that these connecting streets were not implemented, plus the soon-to-arrive Great Depression, set the stage for the Oriental to become something of a "white elephant" in ensuing years. That was ironic because of the fact that elephants were prominent in the theatre design and publicity. (Courtesy OHS OrHi 13208.)

In 1926, Tebbetts and his wife toured much of Europe for six months, gleaning many ideas for his dream palace. Here is a view of the mezzanine lounge, looking toward the men's room entry and one of two very ornate false fireplaces. Initially, programs changed every Saturday. Daily afternoon admission was 25¢ and was 35¢ for evenings, as well as all day Sundays, and holidays. In the basement, a staffed kiddies' playground with swings, merry-go-round, and cribs was located. (Courtesy OHS OrHi 39254.)

A pair of open-mouthed, jewel-eyed dragons were perched aside the grand staircase leading to the mezzanine. Elephants, gargoyles, and other vestiges of East India saturated every corner of the theatre. Much was crafted after the Hindu Temple of Angkor. One could wander about the staircases, lounges, and different levels as if touring another exotic country. (Courtesy Robertson, Hay, and Wallace.)

Curtains and lights could be operated from the projection booth or backstage. The 10-foot-high mask at center of the proscenium had color-changing, illuminated eyes, controlled by the organist. The stage was 33 by 84 feet, bracketed by two immense columns supporting the terraced arch above. Both the orchestra pit and organ loft could be raised or lowered independently from each other. (Courtesy Robertson, Hay, and Wallace.)

The cavernous auditorium is viewed from the stage. Seven dressing rooms were on the mezzanine level, sandwiched between the auditorium and the Weatherly Building to the north (right) of this view. A Knabe grand piano was at the disposal of the Oriental Symphony Orchestra in the pit in front of the stage. The Wurlitzer was a 3-13, style 240, under the control of master organist Glenn Shelley. (Courtesy OHS OrHi 49291.)

The Oriental balcony contained 938 seats. Each side of the auditorium was ringed with seven life-sized elephants atop support columns and six flowing tapestries between. Mayor George Baker, no stranger to show business, formally dedicated the theatre and commented on his recent tour of theatres around the country that he had "seen more expensive houses, but never a more beautiful one." (Courtesy Robertson, Hay, and Wallace.)

This huge auditorium dome held 2,700 lights and measured 46 feet across. Utilizing red, yellow, blue, and clear bulbs on separate circuits, just about any color could be blended. The brass bowl above the chandelier weighed 2,400 pounds. The main chandelier was impressive. It was a 2,000-pound, 12-foot-diameter, 24-foot-high fixture, surrounded by six outstretched smaller lanterns. (Courtesy Robertson, Hay, and Wallace.)

The staircase from the mezzanine leading to the balcony, while at the top of a long climb from the main floor, offered the most spectacular entrance into the auditorium. Nearing the top, one saw nothing but the huge dome and chandelier ahead just before emerging into the center of the balcony. (Courtesy Robertson, Hay, and Wallace.)

CinemaScope arrived in 1953, as well as a new wedge-shaped marquee. When Portland's Civic Auditorium was being renovated in 1965 for two and a half years, the Oriental stage was called back into regular, full service. In fact, many felt that the acoustics were better here. In the late 1960s, there was a special monthly series of silent movies presented with pipe organ accompaniment. (Courtesy Robertson, Hay, and Wallace.)

The Oriental Wurlitzer pipe organ still evokes strong feelings among Portlanders. Notables that played throughout the years were Gaylord Carter and George Wright. In February 1970, a public auction to dispose of the building's contents and furnishings was held. The Wurlitzer was soon relocated to the Organ Grinder Pizza Parlor, where it entertained for decades more. (Courtesy Robert MacNeur.)

This is the end of the Oriental Theatre, as captured on 8-mm home movie film, in April 1970. In the weeks previous, the well-publicized auctioning off of the entire contents and furnishings had been completed. The result is—to this day—many, many Oriental artifacts have been collected and preserved in Portland-area homes. All that remains is a 39-year-old surface parking lot next to the Weatherly Building. (Courtesy OHS OrHi 51650.)

The last of the downtown palaces constructed was the Portland Theatre. It is also the last remaining downtown palace that the city still retains. An announcement was made in late 1926 for Portland's first venue for the Publix theatre chain. Rapp and Rapp, world-renowned theatre designers, were commissioned in association with local architects James DeYoung and Knud Roald. The theatre is of 20th-century Italian Renaissance design. (Courtesy OHS OrHi 47550.)

Combined with the adjacent Heathman Hotel, the complex occupies an entire block on Southwest Broadway, between Salmon and Main Streets, directly opposite where the Broadway Theatre stood. The entrance and lobby occupied 40 by 80 feet and the theatre itself 120 by 180 feet, the largest such footprint in Oregon at the time. Some 700,000 common bricks and 350,000 exterior-facing bricks were used in construction. (Courtesy OHS bb004480.)

Typical of the design for most of the Publix theatres at the time nationwide, no expenses were spared. At the same time, Rapp and Rapp was busy designing its only other Pacific Northwest theatre, the Paramount in Seattle, Washington. The $1,425.00.00 showplace opened March 28, 1928. Opening advertisements promoted "4,000 seats," but at opening, the actual 3,066 count far surpassed that of any other movie house in Portland. (Courtesy Steve Stone.)

On March 13, 1930, it was recommissioned as the Paramount, as were about 40 other chain screens around the country, to solidify corporate imagery. A short-lived feature of the building was a small "try-out theatre" adjacent to the stage on the mezzanine level. It had its own separate dressing rooms, seats for about 50 persons, lighting, and a pair of moving picture projectors. (Courtesy Steve Stone.)

The grand lobby, with a three-story-high ceiling made of silver and gold leaf above mirrored walls, is pictured here. The lobby differed from others in Portland in the fact that it was not carpeted but rather of a tile and marble surface. The theatre was decorated with numerous statues, an illuminated fountain, paintings, and fine furniture, pieces of which were promoted as coming "from private collections around the world." (Courtesy OHS OrHi 68392.)

This is a view of the inner lobby. There were two orchestras for evening performances: one a large, 30-piece symphony in the auditorium and a smaller one for the patrons in the grand lobby. There were four Knabe grand pianos: one in the orchestra pit, one on the stage, and the others in the ladies' rooms. Main restroom lounges, with telephones and phonographs, were in the basement. (Courtesy OHS OrHi 68394.)

The proscenium was 54 feet wide and 32 feet high. The Paramount had a $46,500 Wurlitzer pipe organ, and 14 dressing rooms were available for performers. There were even classrooms for training the vast service staff. In 1932, the Paramount closed because of the Depression. Staying dark for over a year, it reopened November 10, 1933, with some operational changes. Big-time Publix-Leow stage revues were gone for good. (Courtesy OHS OrHi 68409.)

This is a view of the side auditorium wall decor and leading edge of balcony. Above is a "hanging ceiling," which allowed for an atmospheric, indirect lighting effect. Besides staircases, elevators transported patrons to the mezzanine and balcony levels. In the 1950s, a wide screen was installed, allowing presentations in CinemaScope and VistaVision. Touring road shows were still presented into the 1960s. (Courtesy OHS OrHi 68419.)

This and the two following illustrations are of the fund-raising premiere of *This is the Army*, August 18, 1943. The Paramount, as well as other downtown houses, often had spectacular events, even at the opening of rather mediocre programs. It was all part of the flashiness and glamour that was constantly expected. For this event, military vehicles were even positioned in the lobby. (Courtesy Steve Stone.)

The era of glitzy, regular theatre-going such as this would soon be in decline. With fading attendance through the 1960s, movie presentations ended in August 1972. For a while, it housed regular rock concerts, but that trade created a lot of wear. As bookings tapered off, auctions were held of theatre furnishings, including the Wurlitzer. Talk of razing the building abounded, stirring memories of the vanished Oriental Theatre. (Courtesy Steve Stone.)

An effort was started in 1982 by the city to acquire and restore the Paramount. Central to this idea was the stage, which was 30 feet deep and fully equipped. Originally, hydraulic lifts could raise the stage up or down, as well as move it forward or back. The city took over, and a yearlong, $9-million renovation took place, with a reopening in September 1984. (Courtesy Steve Stone.)

So one downtown movie palace has been saved. It is now the 2,776-seat Arlene Schnitzer Concert Hall, home of the Portland Symphony. Free public tours are offered. The 10-ton vertical sign is a 1982 re-creation, with 2,000 ten-watt bulbs and 1,000 feet of neon. Although it is divorced from its birthright of motion pictures now, the building, at least, still survives. (Photograph by Gary Lacher.)

Two

NOT AS DRESSED UP

Many downtown theatres with under 1,000 seating capacity also provided audiences with plenty of entertainment, perhaps with a little less grandeur than their palatial cousins. They provided much needed entertainment, usually at lesser admission prices, and ranged the spectrum from first-run single features or double features of new films to second-run films, usually double features at a greatly reduced price. Finally there were the "grind houses" that ran low-budget films, exploitation, and adult programs, and sometimes at all hours of the day and night. These certainly provided an alternate movie atmosphere for a lesser price. Many began as nickelodeons during the early 1910s, sometimes evolving out of taverns and stores. It was not long, however, until they would be phased out by fairly decent theatres, many showing first-run double features. Although they lacked the substantial atmosphere that people would expect for a first-run downtown show, they stood up to the test of time through several decades, often modernizing marquees and equipment and many times hiding their origins as a nickelodeon. As in the case of the largest theatres, the lesser ones also disappeared, perhaps even more rapidly, especially as a result of television in the 1950s.

The 850-seat, concrete construction Globe Theatre was opened September 12, 1912, at the corner of Southwest Eleventh Avenue and Washington Street. It was one of only two "T-style" houses downtown, the other being the Jefferson Theatre, nearly eight blocks south. Already numerous nickelodeons dotted downtown, but in the 1910s, larger picture houses were focused within one block on either side of Washington Street. (Courtesy OHS bb004486.)

When Seattle, Washington, showman John Hamrick decided to enter the Portland market in 1921, he acquired the Globe. It reopened as the Blue Mouse Theatre, November 28, with *The Queen of Sheba* as the opening fare. Though he was never quite specific about his reasons for naming it the Blue Mouse, it was however, a move he performed in all cities where he opened theatres. (Courtesy OHS bb004485.)

During the 1920s, the Blue Mouse played first-run films frequently. When Vitaphone arrived in Portland, equipment was first placed at the Blue Mouse. On March 25, 1927, ran *Don Juan* plus several Vitaphone shorts. Later *The Jazz Singer* would also have its Portland debut here. By the 1930s, the house was relegated to playing mostly sub-run offerings. In 1941, Hamrick handed over operations of the theatre to Paul Forsythe and partners. (Courtesy OHS bb004473.)

From then on, "the Mouse" was the place to be downtown every Saturday afternoon for hundreds of youngsters. Until the theatre finally closed for good, almost every kid in the city had ventured there at one time or another. Cartoons, serial episodes, and a Western or two were all presented in a more "respected" atmosphere than the area grind houses. (Courtesy OHS bb004488.)

This 1957 view shows the Gerlinger Building on Southwest Washington Street (left), through which Blue Mouse patrons entered. However, the more attractive, theatrical facing on Southwest Eleventh Avenue was never designed or used as an entrance but rather was only the rear exits from the auditorium. Most movie houses along Washington Street were closing, as they were now concentrated on Southwest Broadway. (Courtesy OHS OrHi 53737.)

When the Blue Mouse closed in August 1958, the operator, Paul Forsythe, took a lease on the Capitol Theatre on Southwest Fourth Avenue. The vertical sign and marquee were removed, then trucked the eight blocks to that location, and installed there. The Gerlinger Building and theatre were demolished March 1959 and replaced by a two-story parking garage for the Medical Center Building on Southwest Tenth Avenue. (Courtesy www.HistoricPhotoArchive.com.)

The nine-story Studio Building (left), at Southwest Ninth and Taylor Streets, was constructed in 1927 to exclusively house musicians and artists. Luther Lee Dougan was the architect. Besides the 128 soundproofed studios, an adjoining 450-seat recital theatre (right) was constructed on the north side. The building was never fully occupied before the Depression struck, necessitating some changes. (Photograph by Gary Lacher.)

By 1930, the recital hall was named the Studio Theatre, occasionally blending in film programs. In 1932, regular movies became the staple of the now Taylor Street Theatre. The entrance was through the main building's Taylor Street entry. In September 1947, it was taken over by J. J. Parker and began operation under the Guild name. This is a view from May 1950. The entrance was moved around the corner onto Ninth Avenue. (Courtesy www.HistoricPhotoArchive.com.)

For the next 20 years, the house specialized in foreign and art films. With the entrance on Southwest Ninth Avenue now, the theatre had the unusual layout of patrons entering the auditorium at the front, on either side of the screen, then proceeding upward to the rear loge sections. The lobby was in an area that was once the stage. (Courtesy Gary Fine Collection.)

In 1977, the Guild began running classics exclusively, a format that had been only dabbled in here as well as other cinemas. Installed was 16-mm equipment, as more classics were available in that format. Soon festivals evolved, such as Hitchcock, Tracy and Hepburn, *The Thin Man*, and the most popular, an annual James Bond 007 showcase. (Courtesy Gary Fine Collection.)

The interior complemented the classics as well. Auditorium walls depicted the famous Hollywood sign in California and a vintage cameraman, and overhead were hundreds of twinkling "stars." Intermission music was selected by patrons on a lobby jukebox containing 200 movie and television themes and songs. After a decade, and the advent of videotape and cable television, the Guild abandoned classics and went back to sub-run programs. (Courtesy Gary Fine Collection.)

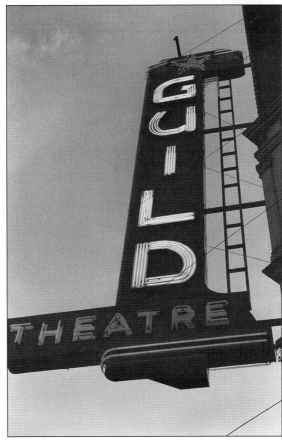

It stopped running regular feature films in 1998 and was downtown's last such single-screen venue. It continued to be used for several more years as presentation facilities for the Northwest Film Study Center. It is now sitting vacant, surrounded by rising and encroaching shadows of new skyscrapers, awaiting a seemingly inevitable fate. The vintage 1947 vertical sign still hangs but now bears the name of a restaurant beneath. (Courtesy Gary Fine Collection.)

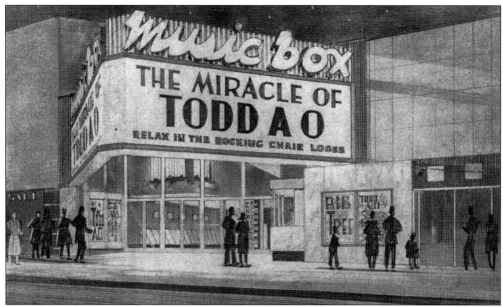

A new Music Box Theatre opened next to the Fox Theatre on Southwest Broadway, near Yamhill Street, in January 1960. This was Portland's sixth and last venue with that name and also John Hamrick's last and only remaining house in the city. It had the smooth, graceful design that was the forerunner to the multiplex look. Aside from the canopy of the marquee, the facade was essentially an entire wall of glass. (Courtesy Steve Stone.)

It was designed specifically for road show presentations. A 35/70-mm projection booth was on the main floor, under the balcony. *Ben Hur* was the first feature to open at the Music Box. This illustration is an artist's faithful projection of what the theatre lobby looked like when completed. The manager's office was inside the sliding glass window behind the planter above the concession counter. (Courtesy Steve Stone.)

78

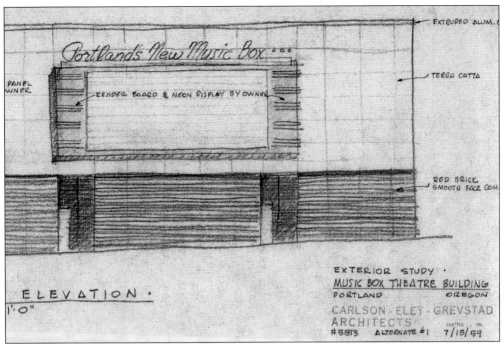

Portland's New Music Box...

PANEL
WNER

READER BOARD & NEON DISPLAY BY OWNER

EXTRUDED ALUM.

TERRA COTTA

RED BRICK
SMOOTH FACE COM.

EXTERIOR STUDY ·
MUSIC BOX THEATRE BUILDING
PORTLAND   OREGON

CARLSON · ELEY · GREVSTAD
ARCHITECTS   SEATTLE   WA.
#5813   ALTERNATE #1   7/15/59

ELEVATION ·
1'-0"

This is the accurate rendering of a secondary reader board installed on the Yamhill Street end of the building. The firm of Carlson-Eley-Grevstad designed the 628-seat cinema. With Hamrick's 1959 closure of the Liberty Theatre four blocks away, seats, carpeting, and other fixtures were moved here and installed. Much of the theatre was created out of the transformation of a quarter-block collection of 1924 storefronts. Radical at the time was the fact that there was no stage at all. The waterfall title curtain lowered right to the auditorium floor, 15 feet in front of the first row. (Courtesy Steve Stone.)

Thoughts were given in the 1970s to merge the Music Box and adjacent Fox into a single operation and possibly add two additional screens in the Fox balcony. That never happened. Both were still separate, single-screen operations when they closed in September 1990. The curtain was brought down for the last time on the 70-year history of the Music Box name in Portland, having graced six different structures. Currently, the 27-story Fox Tower occupies the block. (Courtesy Gary Fine Collection.)

The 300-seat Princess Theatre, located on Northwest Sixth Avenue at West Burnside Street, opened May 1911. It was a typical "shooting gallery, semi-fireproof picture show," one of many constructed that year and first of the new fire-code compliant structures for movies downtown. This view is from around 1923, when the Sax Amusement Company was running it. In 1939, it became the Star but was sometimes known as the Four-Star or New Star. (Courtesy OHS Delano/Acme 7445-28.)

From about 1940 until it closed around 1975, it embarked upon what started as "burlesque" films, evolving by the late 1960s into strictly a porno house. This view, from November 1954, shows how it looked throughout that era. It is now used as a nightclub venue, with seating removed and interior obliterated. However, the exterior facade is still nearly completely original, except for a new, decorative marquee-style awning. (Courtesy www.HistoricPhotoArchive.com.)

The Casino Theatre on right and the barely visible Burnside Theatre across the street were a block away from the Star, fronting West Burnside Street, between Fourth and Fifth Avenues, about 1928. All were working-class houses. The Casino was built in 1913 with seats for 624, plus a seldom-used full stage. The Burnside was built in 1914 and seated 500. Both closed in 1930 to be demolished for the widening of West Burnside. (Courtesy OHS COP00759.)

Neither house saw sound. However, here is a rare view inside the Burnside Theatre of the Powers 6A silent machines with vertical arc lamps. These early "lamp" or "machine rooms" were cramped, stuffy, and hot affairs and not without many hazards, such as the nitrate film itself. Such projection booths would become even more crowded with the coming of talkies. (Courtesy Dick Prather.)

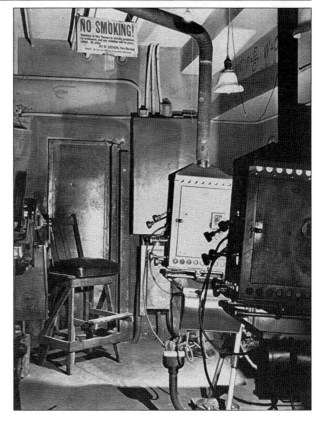

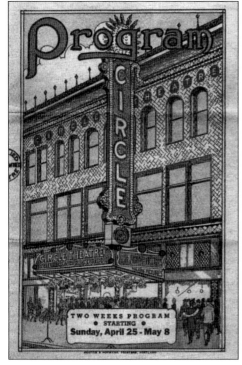

Built exclusively for motion pictures, the 800-seat Circle Theatre, seen here around 1918, was on Southwest Fourth Avenue, just south of Washington Street. David C. Lewis was the architect. Opening December 1912, it was known by the slogan "The People's Theatre," memorialized in a circular, metal emblem in the sidewalk out front. (Courtesy OHS OrHi 102278.)

This is a 1942 program for the Circle Theatre. It was a sub-run, double-feature, economy house, and open all night most of its life, like the block-away Capitol and Round-Up. All three "grind houses" changed features three times a week all the way to closure. The Circle closed in 1963 and was demolished the following year for a parking structure and retail. (Courtesy Don Nelson.)

The last theatre constructed downtown prior to the multiplex era was the Capitol Theatre, opening July 20, 1929. Lee Thomas and Albert Mercier designed it for talking pictures and vaudeville, and it was of a modified Spanish design. This would also be Portland's last vaudeville house, and it never rivaled any of the larger (and better) offerings up on Broadway. It had 778 seats, including a balcony. (Courtesy OHS OrHi 51828.)

This view is of the Capitol, on Southwest Fourth Avenue at Morrison Street, as it appeared in January 1931. By the 1950s, vaudeville was nothing more than striptease. Stripper Tempest Storm even ran it for a spell. The Capitol closed in 1957 and was sold the following year to Paul Forsythe, operator of the Blue Mouse Theatre. Since that house was soon to be torn down, he took a lease on the Capitol and then moved the Blue Mouse vertical and marquee to this site. (Courtesy OHS bb004474.)

Pictured here in 1972 is the Blue Mouse that existed until January 1977. The Blue Mouse and the Round-Up around the corner on Southwest Morrison Street were Portland's last all-night grind houses. The entire block is now a parking structure with retail mix. However, the neon lettering shown was rescued and now hangs in the one-time auditorium of another movie house in northwest Portland. (Photograph by Steve Stone.)

The 300-seat Rex Theatre, located on Southwest Morrison Street, between Third and Fourth Avenues, opened in a converted storefront space of the Alisky Building in 1916. It was no different in appearance or operation from the two dozen or so nickelodeons of the 1908–1920 period. It did, however, hold the distinction of having the city's very first licensed theatre sign, permit No. 243, issued March 17, 1916. (Courtesy OHS R-25.)

But it took on its most famous identity in 1947, when local showman Ted Gamble added it to his string of movie houses, redecorating it completely in an Old West theme and reopening as the Round-Up Theatre. The policy was to play nothing but Western features and serials. Chandeliers were made of suspended wagon wheels, wood paneling abounded inside and out, and the vintage wooden nickelodeon seats blended with that theme. (Courtesy Steve Stone.)

The supporting clientele remained much as it had always been: low-income tenants of the borderline skid-row area. Quaint as it was, it quickly reverted to a triple-feature, grind house with an all-night policy until the very end in early 1977. The entire block is now a multi-story parking garage with retail stores on the ground level. (Photograph by Steve Stone.)

In 1922, the 300-seat Union Theatre was constructed at West Burnside Street and Southwest Third Avenue. Francis Jacobberger was the architect. Mainly a grind house, it did offer second-rate vaudeville in addition to moving pictures for many years. When Third Avenue was widened in 1930, the front 30 feet of the building was cut off, resulting in this facade. It also was given the name 3rd Avenue Theatre. In 1963, it became the Paris and began a 16-year stint as an X-rated house. (Photograph by Gary Lacher.)

It then was home for two decades to local drama groups before closing. Recently, it reopened as a video-projection porno house once again. The modest, 15-foot-tall vertical sign dates to 1938, making it the oldest surviving such theatre sign downtown. The 1940 reader board is the oldest such sign still functioning in the entire city. No vintage interior features remain, and seating has been drastically reduced. (Photograph by Gary Lacher.)

Three

LOST IN THE NEIGHBORHOODS

The history of Portland's growing neighborhoods reflects the history of the movie theatres. It is hard to imagine today that there were dozens of individual movie theatres throughout the city as early as 1915. The movie industry reflects Portland's growth during the early 1910s, and 1911 was a boom year for theatre growth. At that time, going to a movie meant perhaps a half hour to hour of entertainment. Many programs were short, with brief two-reel melodramas and comedies filling the program, no more than a half hour to an hour. With the rapid growth of East Portland, local businesspersons quickly set up small buildings for the movies. By the time longer feature film presentation began appearing after 1913, theatre going became more of an evening's worth of entertainment, and neighborhood theatres began growing in size and comfort. Instead of a single piano, the newer theatres could provide a decent organ and perhaps some musicians. Although there are a surprising number of theatre buildings still in existence, some still as movie houses, many have vanished and only building structures survive, as trendy new stores or auto garages. Sadly, some have been torn down when they could have been renovated back into a movie theatre or at least a place of community events. Besides those included here, Portland has at least two dozen other nickelodeon and neighborhood structures, such as the former Aero, Echo, Esquire, and Multnomah, to name a few.

The oldest Portland structure still standing that once housed a nickelodeon is this 1891 landmark three-story building at Southeast Grand Avenue and Washington Street. City directories list the Grand Avenue Theatre from 1909 through 1915. Seating likely was less than 300. The building originally was a mortuary, with apartments above. Currently a bank occupies the main floor. (Photograph by Gary Lacher.)

The Brownie Theater ran only briefly, from June 1911 into 1912. Near Foster Road on Southeast Sixty-seventh Avenue, it likely had just 300 seats. Part of a local 1911 trend, the projection room was a small, separate concrete room attached to the rear of the structure, accessed only by an outside stairway and door. The structure has been used mostly for repairs and storage since. (Photograph by Gary Lacher.)

By 1910, neighborhood picture houses, like downtown nickelodeons, were rapidly evolving into a style of their own. Such is the Star Theatre, located at Southeast Thirteenth Avenue and Spokane Street. Seating was probably only for about 250, and it operated until about 1920. The facade still displays original cast-stone, concrete blocks, while the original theatre floor remains hidden beneath that of Gino's Pizza, the current tenant. (Courtesy Sellwood-Moreland Improvement League.)

The first movie house on Northeast Sandy Boulevard was the 320-seat Elite, at Forty-seventh Avenue. Designed by Roberts and Roberts, it opened in 1912. Later it was the Rose City Park, then the Rose City, closing in 1922. The exterior of this building remarkably still conveys the early "picture show" look, but the interior has all been altered. For over 40 years, it has been Pal's Shanty Tavern. (Photograph by Gary Lacher.)

The 375-seat Crest Theatre stood at North Lombard Street near Portsmouth Avenue in 1968, awaiting demolition. Part of the 1911 explosion of Portland's "semi-fireproof" construction, it opened as the Portsmouth, becoming the Crest in 1937. The facade reflected the building intent accurately, but the interior was of plain, concrete walls, punctuated by pilasters and arches. Author Steve Stone gained his roots of movie going and theatre appreciation here. (Courtesy Steve Stone.)

Five days after the Portsmouth permit was issued (July 17, 1911), the same contractor and architect obtained permits to build the Woodlawn Theatre, on Northeast Dekum Street at Durham Avenue. Aside from a different style facade, the two theatres were completely identical. In 1929, not able to make it into the "talkie" era, it was converted into commercial space. Currently, a new owner is poised to renovate the building. (Photograph by Gary Lacher.)

The still very vintage-looking 300-seat Ideal Theater sits at the northwest corner of Thurman Street and Twenty-fourth Avenue. Emil Schact and Son were the 1912 architects. It became the Senate in 1927; Bluebird in 1929 following a fire; Elmo in 1944; and Crown in 1951 until closing December 1953. Inside, the actual neon marquee lighting from the Blue Mouse marquee is mounted on a wall. (Photograph by Gary Lacher.)

The original Ideal name still adorns the Twenty-fourth Avenue exterior of the building. An oddity of the building is that it has a parallelogram footprint, not a square or rectangle. This is due to a slight eastward shift in the rear property lines, not noticeable by sight but very present in plot maps and the blueprints. Currently, a photography studio occupies the theater. (Photograph by Gary Lacher.)

The Alhambra Theatre opened January 1914 and was one of W. E. Tebbetts's early operations. Hiram E. Irish was the architect. Located on Southeast Hawthorne Boulevard at Forty-ninth Avenue, it was renovated to become the 480-seat Mount Tabor in 1934. A small second screen was later constructed. Regular movies ceased in 1990. It has since been gutted out to but a few auditorium details for a live music club. (Photograph by Gary Lacher.)

In 1912, a 300-seat nickelodeon house opened at Northeast Eighteenth Avenue and Alberta Street as the Victoria. In 1923, Lee Thomas crafted it into this 660-seat, L-shaped venue. The original auditorium was now the lobby and rear foyer. A balcony, mezzanine foyer, cry room, and organ were added during this $75,000 renovation. Amazingly, today it still retains all these visible features, except seats. (Courtesy OHS OrHi 68407.)

In 1930, it reopened under the Alberta name with sound. It last ran movies in 1965 and has since been home to a series of churches. This c. 1930 view also captures much detail, including light fixtures, still present. The wall tapestries have been painted over. This nearly pristine interior now sits idle, awaiting plans by a new owner to convert to a small retail mall. (Courtesy OHS OrHi 68411.)

March 1924 saw the debut of the Bob White Theatre, on Southeast Foster Road near Sixty-fifth Avenue. Its namesake was a local showman, long associated with Multnomah Theatres, which dominated the suburban field in 1920s Portland. Thomas Lee crafted the 712-seat house. Closing in 1986, it now houses a private collection of pipe organ artifacts. Two former silent-era theatres sit on either side of the Bob White as well. (Courtesy OHS bb004472.)

This 375-seat, "shooting gallery"–style Rio Theatre was located on North Mississippi Avenue near Failing Street. Construction began September 1911 and was completed in March 1912 as the Gay Theatre. Becoming the Rio in 1934, it closed in 1956 and was later demolished. This view is from around 1950 and captures the popularity that neighborhood houses still had. (Courtesy Donald Myrick.)

The 688-seat Alameda Theatre opened May 1926 and was designed by Walter E. Kelly. Located at Northeast Thirtieth Avenue and Alberta Street, it was long known as the 30th Avenue. The auditorium contains Portland's only "atmospheric-style" skyline and building imagery. In the 1970s, it was a popular "blaxploitation" house. Currently it is the Victory Outreach Temple. (Courtesy OHS OrHi 75067.)

The 750-seat Chaldean Theatre on North Denver Avenue at Schofield Street opened September 17, 1925. It was described as being of California mission–style design. Architectural plans were by Richard A. Miller. It became the Kenton in March 1930, reflecting the community name, and operated continuously until May 1957. It now houses an auto-repair facility, with parts of the sealed-off balcony and booth the only interior features still intact. (Courtesy OHS bb004475.)

Earl G. Cash designed this theatre—a 620-seat Colonial, located on North Albina Avenue near Killingsworth Street, which opened November 1924. It operated until 1963, closed for seven years, then reopened briefly in 1970. From 1973, it housed a church until demolished in 2000 for expansion of the adjacent college. Along with vintage acoustical wall tapestries still in the auditorium, a nearby 1909-era former nickelodeon was also demolished. (Photograph by Steve Stone.)

The 640-seat Irvington Theater, located at Northeast Broadway and Fourteenth Avenue, operated for 65 years, opening in September 1924. This 1928 view shows the unusual angled entrance. The 1930 widening of Northeast Broadway eliminated that feature. In October 1990, the theater closed and turned into a restaurant and specialty shops. Only the vintage Irvington vertical sign remains, restored in 1992 as a neighborhood icon. (Courtesy OHS OrHi 03283.)

The 700-seat Granada Theater sat at Northeast Seventy-seventh Avenue and Glisan Street. Opening August 24, 1924, it was described as reflecting a Moorish design. Architect Earl G. Cash designed the building. After the Granada closed in October 1957, it began being used by churches. Four other former northeast Portland theatres have been similarly rescued and converted since the 1960s—there is something to be said about "being saved." (Courtesy OHS bb004477.)

This is Graeper's Egyptian Theatre, around 1932, on Northeast Union Avenue (now Martin Luther King Boulevard) at Russell Street. Opening September 27, 1924, the facade had to be pushed back 10 feet for the widening of the street in 1930, but it retained its original look exactly. Illuminated steam vapor vented from the two finials above the facade at night in the early years. (Courtesy www.HistoricPhotoArchive.com.)

This was the dream of William Adolph Graeper, containing an Egyptian motif replete with abundant hieroglyphics throughout the house. Edward A. Miller was the architect. There were 866 seats on the main floor and 344 in the balcony. After closing in April 1963, it became a warehouse. Following a $3-million renovation in 1992, it is now the New Song Church. (Courtesy Graeper Family Collection.)

The 682-seat Sellwood Theatre is on Southeast Tacoma Street near Milwaukie Avenue. It was the first show house constructed for the local Moyer family, part of Portland's theatre scene since 1919. It opened April 6, 1938, replacing their earlier theatre around the corner. Day W. Hillborn was the architect of this art deco design. It closed in February 1997 and is now a Columbia Sportswear Factory Outlet store. (Courtesy Bob Kane.)

The Ames Theatre on Southeast Foster Road near Fifty-fourth Avenue was constructed to replace the next-door 1915-era Star Theatre. James W. De Young designed the 500-seat Ames, which opened October 30, 1936. It last operated in May 1966. Afterward, the two connected buildings were long the Day Music Company and held frequent public music recitals in the former theatre auditorium. (Courtesy Day Music Company.)

Four

THE SURVIVORS

Luckily, there are the survivors. Movies will never cease to entertain, and in the case of numerous Portland Theatres, they seem to be as durable as their product. These are the venerable places of entertainment that are still standing and that have spent all or most of their existence as movie screen venues. Some have run continuously since the 1910s, such as the Clinton, a small theatre successfully catering to an eclectic audience. The Moreland, in southeast Portland, remains architecturally the same as when it opened and still as a single-screen theatre. Others survive after going through many stages of names and closings, such as the CineMagic, which began as the Palm Theatre in 1913. The Cinema 21 still has single-screen movie presentations, with an opening curtain to match, showing specialty film programs. The Avalon, beginning as the Sunnyside in 1912, still brings in people for movies. The Roseway, recently refurbished, has been entertaining since 1924. The Academy, closed for several years, has been reborn as a triplex. It was originally opened in 1948. The strength of these examples has been the neighborhoods of Portland. With the refurbished growth of the inner communities, new populations and families have given Portland a continuing chance for theatres to not only survive, but to entertain its citizens in the same manner as on those rainy nights of 80 years ago.

The Avalon, on Southeast Belmont Street near Thirty-fourth Avenue, is Portland's oldest operating movie house, opening the first week of August 1912 as the Sunnyside Theatre. It was Portland's first L-shaped theatre, containing 425 seats and a small orchestra pit, still intact today. The proscenium is molded plaster with a ring of electric light sockets, which in recent years has been reactivated. In 1935, it became the Avalon. (Photograph by Steve Stone.)

Early in 1958, the Avalon initiated the triple-feature format in programming to Portland neighborhood screens. In 1972, an adjacent storefront was converted to a second auditorium. Later a third was added. Now the main auditorium is a huge video arcade game room, the Wunderland Arcade. The two smaller screens still offer recent movies. The distinctive vertical sign dates to 1949. (Photograph by Gary Lacher.)

The 300-seat Clinton Street Theatre sits at the corner of Southeast Twenty-sixth Avenue and Clinton Street. Designed by Charles A. Duke in 1913, it is Portland's second oldest operating movie house. The entrance faced Twenty-sixth Avenue until 1922. Once known as the 26th Avenue and the Encore, it became the Clinton on May 30, 1975. Shortly afterward, it played *Rocky Horror Picture Show*, which has now been shown every weekend since. (Photograph by Gary Lacher.)

The 449-seat Palm Theatre, at Southeast Twentieth Avenue and Hawthorne Boulevard, was noted in permits as being completed in December 1913. That makes it the third oldest operating movie theatre in the city. It also is noted for its many name changes, being Hawthorne (1915), Star (1931), Star Hawthorne (1932), Zephyr (1937), Plaza (1938), Fine Arts (1957), Columbia Repertory (1986), and finally CineMagic (1991). Today it holds 275 seats. (Courtesy OHS OrHi 102704.)

The theatre was gutted in 1916 to convert to a garage, but plans were quickly abandoned; the refurnished theatre was back up and running in 1917. Originally, it had a "T"-type entrance, which by 1937 became the current "L" style. It was an art house from 1957 until 1986, and then it became a live drama venue. In the year 1991, the venue saw a complete makeover to reopen as the CineMagic, presenting classic movies. (Courtesy Gary Fine Collection.)

A brand-new, 1950s retro-look marquee was erected, 70-mm projectors installed, the drama stage removed, and this floor-length, wraparound title curtain crafted. Auditorium seating was reduced to a more comfortable 275. When the movie starts, the curtain disappears completely behind the screen. Since, it has returned to first-run and sub-run offerings. (Courtesy Gary Fine Collection.)

The 730-seat State Theatre, at Northwest Twenty-first Avenue and Hoyt Street, opened February 1925. A locally manufactured William Wood pipe organ was installed, and William's brother, L. D. Wood, was the organist. Other Wood installations were at the original Sellwood, Jefferson, and Oregon Theatres. The original architect is unknown, but in 1941, Lee A. Thomas redesigned it to become the 21st Avenue. Since 1962, it has been the Cinema 21. (Courtesy OHS OrHi 26913.)

The 750-seat Oregon Theatre faces Southeast Division Street at Marguerite Avenue and is a typical mid-1920s single-floor house. It opened September 4, 1925, and was designed by Hubert A. Williams. It holds a historical record, not often acknowledged publicly. It is the longest running X-rated porno house in Portland, since 1970. Of the 13 city movie houses that once offered such fare, only two remain. (Photograph by Gary Lacher.)

The Laurelhurst Theater opened November 1, 1923, on Northeast Twenty-eighth Street. It was a new, larger breed of the early 1920s, being 60 feet wide and 120 feet long when built. The single auditorium seated 650 people. Charles W. Ertz was the architect. On Christmas Day 1938, a larger 80-foot-long lobby extension facing East Burnside Street opened. The space might have originally been intended to be a very early second auditorium. (Photograph by Gary Lacher.)

This is the vintage 1949 vertical sign and marquee. The neon tubing in the sign, as well as imbedded in the building facade, has been faithfully maintained. The 29.5-foot-high, 500-pound vertical sign was removed for restoration in 2008 and is now back in place. The main auditorium has been halved down the middle to create another screen and two storefronts in front converted into another two auditoriums. (Photograph by Gary Lacher.)

The tile-clad box office still is relatively unaltered from the 1938 reopening. It is typical of what was once a common look of many theatres and is still in use every day. In 2000, new operators renovated and reopened the theater to the successful theater/pub it is today. Although seating had to be changed, other items, such as a large, long-hidden lobby mirror, have been returned to use. (Photograph by Steve Stone.)

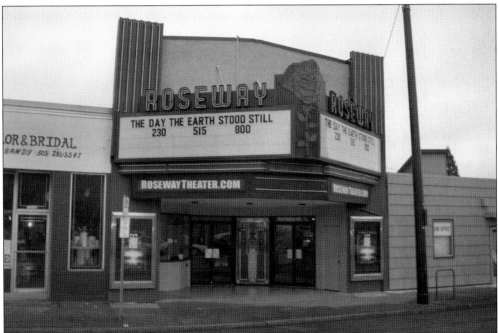

Hubert A. Williams was the architect for the 800-seat Roseway Theater. Located at Northeast Sandy Boulevard and Seventy-second Avenue, it opened November 1924. Long a neighborhood venue, it became a showcase for classic revival films in 1979. A Robert Morton pipe organ was even installed briefly at this time. In 2008, the theatre was extensively renovated into a one-screen, state-of-the-art, first-run house. (Photograph by Gary Lacher.)

The 750-seat Venetian Theatre, designed by Edward A. Miller, opened in March 1925 at North Lombard Street and Alta Avenue. This is the only "diagonal theatre" ever constructed in Portland. The entrance is on one corner and the screen at the opposite corner of the building. It was renamed the St. Johns in 1936, reflecting the neighborhood name. (Courtesy OHS OrHi 91143.)

In 1925, the Venetian had the largest Wurlitzer pipe organ in Portland except for the one at the Liberty Theatre downtown. The organ grille was uniquely placed above the proscenium. It was one of very few neighborhood houses to have a ramp to the balcony as well as a staircase. The balcony is now a second theatre, with both showing first-run films and serving pizza and wines. (Courtesy OHS bb004484.)

Ike Geller opened this theatre, bearing his name, on Christmas Day, 1927. It is located near the intersection of Southeast Powell Boulevard and Milwaukie Avenue, in the Brooklyn neighborhood. Ike's first theater was 1923's Walnut Park in northeast Portland. This one was much more in line with the classic designs of the "Golden 20s" neighborhood show houses. The architect was Edward A. Miller. (Courtesy OHS OrHi 91271.)

The 630-seat house was renamed the Aladdin in 1934, a name it still bears today. It ran for over 30 years as a porno house, with *Deep Throat* playing for 14 of them. In 1991, it was revived into a classic movie and performing arts house. The interior still looks as it did in 1927, including stage, chandeliers, and organ grilles. Movies are not currently shown, as it concentrates now on musical arts. (Photograph by Mike Mathews.)

The Moreland Theater, on Southeast Milwaukie Avenue near Bybee Street, was designed in a Spanish style by Thomas and Thomas and opened September 10, 1925. Here we see its 26-foot-high vertical sign, representing a huge colored fountain, as it looked that October. It originally had 641 seats. Its motto when it opened—"The Successful Theatre Satisfies it's Patrons"—still holds true after 80 years of continuous operation. (Courtesy OHS bb004490.)

The former pipe organ grilles, shown here in 1925, can still be seen today, but the pipes and Robert Morton console have long since been removed. The Moreland retained Portland's very last vintage movie house love seats until 2000. This auditorium was featured in the fire scene in the 1990s movie *Come See the Paradise*. The nearby Clinton Street Theatre was also featured in scenes. (Courtesy OHS bb004489.)

The Hollywood Theater on opening day, Saturday, July 17, 1926, was met with crowds and festivities galore. The Hollywood was described as being in the style of 18th-century Italian, with an influence of Spanish design. It was designed by Bennes and Herzog for the Jensen and von Herberg theater chain and located on Northeast Sandy Boulevard at Forty-first Avenue. Soon the district itself would take on the name of the theatre. (Courtesy Film Action Oregon.)

The distinctive rococo tower is a landmark visible from much of the Sandy Boulevard stretch. The Hollywood theatre was promoted as having cost $500,000 to build and seated 1,491 patrons. This is the original box office, removed during the Cinerama conversion in 1961. Now there is a separate cashier window to the right of these doors. (Courtesy Film Action Oregon.)

This is just inside the front doors. The shape is still the same, but the entire decor has been altered and doors replaced. However, the original exit sign is still intact. Walter E. Tebbetts was the first manager for the Hollywood, coming here from the nearby Highway Theatre just closing. In little more than a year, he would next take the helm of the new Oriental Theatre. (Courtesy OHS bb004482.)

The main lobby in 1926, looking at the staircase to the mezzanine, is much the same today. When the stairs reach a landing midway up, a tunneled ramp ascends the rest of the way. The theatre was initially a first-run house but by the 1930s was relegated to sub-run and, by the 1950s, was a neighborhood venue. In 1959, things changed with the introduction first of the Cinamiracle wide-screen projection system. (Courtesy Film Action Oregon.)

Next came the three-projector Cinerama system, developed and introduced in 1952, made its Oregon appearance with the debut of *This is Cinerama* at the Hollywood, November 21, 1961. The theater had been renovated at a cost of $125,000, and two additional projection booths were placed in side corners of the auditorium, still visible today. This mezzanine lounge was outfitted with a second concession counter during the Cinerama conversion. (Courtesy Film Action Oregon.)

Here is the original proscenium arch, hidden behind the main auditorium screen. Recently, backstage dressing rooms have been restored to use. Vaudeville was once a key program ingredient when the theater opened. The theater originally had a magnificent $40,000 Wurlitzer pipe organ. Years later, it was removed and relocated to the Imperial Roller Rink. There are plans afoot to install a Wurlitzer here once again. (Courtesy Film Action Oregon.)

Much of this wall decor still exists, in a deteriorating mode, behind drapery that was added when the theatre was converted to Cinerama in 1961. Not fully visible in this image is a distinctive sunburst decoration above the proscenium. False box-seat bays are depicted on the auditorium walls. (Courtesy Film Action Oregon.)

Auditorium chandeliers were a casualty of Cinerama. After the Cinerama thrill had faded, a different tactic was needed to keep up daily attendance. The balcony was turned into two separate auditoriums in 1976, trying to keep up with the proliferation of multiplexes springing up everywhere. The theater changed hands and became just a sub-run, $1.50-a-seat bargain theater. Maintenance ceased. But a rescue effort did eventually organize. (Courtesy Film Action Oregon.)

This is the original Hollywood Theatre orchestra, but the men's individual identities and positions are not specified. The theatre utilized an eight-piece orchestra under the direction of Samuel Soble. The head organist was Robert Clark, but on opening night, the honors were performed by Cecil Teague of the Majestic Theatre downtown. Two months later, Teague would be the inaugural organist at the opening of the Broadway Theatre. (Courtesy OHS OrHi 45752.)

In 1997, the Hollywood was purchased by the Oregon Film and Video Foundation. Since then, a slow but steady effort has been made to obtain funds and contributions to restore the theater. Had this effort not happened, the theater would not be standing here anymore. The Hollywood has a number of hidden treasures, which, given time and money, may well be seen by the public again. (Photograph by Gary Lacher.)

The Hollywood vertical sign, recently refurbished, was not part of the original construction but was added around March 1934. It is 31 feet high, weighs 1,000 pounds, and cost $565 when new. Then the white letters were outlined with blue neon, with a black background and an orange border around the sign edge, combined with chasing 25-watt bulbs. The Hollywood is a bright reminder of something finally saved in Portland. (Photograph by Gary Lacher.)

Lee Thomas and Albert Mercier designed this 1,396-seat theatre, the Bagdad, at Southeast Thirty-seventh Avenue and Hawthorne Boulevard, which opened February 16, 1927. The 100-by-165-foot, reinforced concrete, Italian Renaissance–style theatre featured a red clay tile roof, rounded blind-arch windows, and significant recessed relief sides. A huge electric sign stood atop the roof for several years, able to be seen nearly 10 miles away at night. (Courtesy OHS OrHi 45753.)

The Bagdad and Hollywood Theatres were the only outlying houses to have full stage facilities. The Bagdad's was 28 feet deep, and the fly-loft was 74 feet high. It was the last Portland neighborhood movie house having vaudeville, until August 1948. Then-owner Paul Forsythe booked some of the minor-name acts that were playing at his Capitol Theatre downtown, such as Al Morrison, Betty Reeve, Chester Calhoun, and Artie Jaxon. (Courtesy OHS OrHi 47751.)

The Bagdad in 1974 divided into two theatres; then in 1979, the stage was turned into a third screen, the Backstage Theatre. On May 16, 1991, Brian and Mike McMenamin reopened the Bagdad as one of their brewpub theatres. The concrete wall separating the balcony theatre from the main floor was removed, opening up the entire auditorium once again. Currently, there are seats for 700. (Courtesy OHS OrHi83061.)

The Academy Theatre, on Southeast Stark Street at Seventy-eighth Avenue, was designed by James W. De Young. It was one of the few neighborhood houses constructed after the 1920s. The 637-seat theatre opened April 29, 1948, having rare reverse-incline seating. Closing in 1977, it served two decades as a printing plant. Reopening March 6, 2006, the interior now houses three screens and has revitalized the surrounding neighborhood. (Courtesy Teeny family.)

Five

SOME FINAL SCENES

Through the years, Portland's theatres changed with the times. The post–World War II period of drive-in movies became popular. Then television came in the early 1950s and defined the survivors. New technologies such as CinemaScope, 3-D, stereophonic sound, and other enticements helped keep movies afloat, something television could not do in those categories. Actually, smaller theatres found the costs for modern technical conversions prevented them from continuing. Declining neighborhoods and the flight to the suburbs did not help. Some new outlying theatres were built with several auditoriums, making it more efficient and practical for showing films. The Eastgate and Lloyd Cinema theatres actually had large auditoriums, reminiscent of former downtown houses.

Although downtown Portland has only one remaining original palatial structure, which now serves as a performing arts center, the diversity and fabric of the city's lifestyles and neighborhoods have preserved and provided a new infusion of movie entertainment. Although some traditional single-screen places still exist close to their original movie-going concept, new trends and concepts have modified the showmanship without lessening the entertainment. The respect for architecture and history has provided new ideas for movie shows. Portland has paved the way for the brewpub concept, taking an older theatre, school auditorium, tavern, or any building that will work, and converting it to a place of complete living room entertainment with a shared audience. With a pizza and beer, people can still enjoy a first-run film—getting away from the television set. Families are also given special hours for the movies. This benefits the audience, of course, but also brings back to life the original idea of entertainment from many years ago, even in the same surroundings that earlier generations enjoyed. New technologies, of course, have always enhanced the movie experience, with new digital picture and sound, IMAX, and even a revised 3-D. The latest multiplexes boast of stadium-style seating. Of course, many of these innovations have replaced the live orchestra, opening and closing curtains, live stage shows, and palatial settings. Portland's film community today consists of museums, film festivals, studies programs, and many smaller showings around town.

Interestingly, in some ways, Portland has returned to smaller gatherings similar to 1911. But wherever the gatherings, people will always want to escape for those few hours of another experience: the movies.

The Eastgate Twin Theater was a milestone in Portland's theater history. It opened October 26, 1966, ushering in the era of multiplexes. The reader board was the area's largest in 1966. Each side measured 40 by 34 feet. This would be the flagship for the development of Thomas P. Moyer's Luxury Theaters chain, which would evolve into one of the nation's largest theater operators at 293 screens. (Courtesy Peter Corvallis.)

Martin Bloom and Associates designed the Eastgate. An identical sister theater, the Westgate in Beaverton, would open the following year. In 1972, the area's first three-screen venue, the Jantzen Beach Tri-Cinema, opened, followed in short order by the four-screen Southgate Quad. When even larger theatres grew popular, additional auditoriums were added to most of these early styles. Most were constructed of concrete tilt-up walls, much like warehouses. (Courtesy Peter Corvallis.)

Soon multiple-screen concepts spread to competitors as well, such as Larry Moyer's Cini-Mini Theater, now the Fifth Avenue Cinema. The age of constructing single-screen theaters was over in the practical sense, even though a few more were built, such as the Valley and the Village. But within five years, they too were forced to add additional auditoriums to be able to compete. (Courtesy Peter Corvallis.)

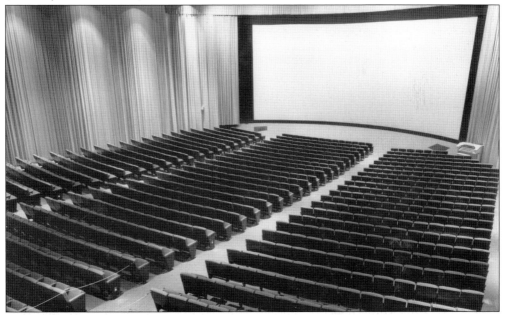

The large Eastgate auditorium originally had 1,300 seats, a massive 82-foot-wide, 30-foot-high screen, and all loge-style rocking chair seating. The smaller theater had 500 seats all grouped together in one section called a "Continental seating arrangement." The Eastgate closed in February 2001, as have most other 1970s and 1980s multiplexes. It is currently a church facility. (Courtesy Peter Corvallis.)

Brian and Mike McMenamin started their noted micro-brew business in 1983, along with renovating numerous historic buildings into drinking establishments. This is their 1912 former Swedish Tabernacle Church building, located on Northwest Glisan Street near Sixteenth Avenue. In 1987, they turned it into the Mission Theater, their very first brewpub theatre, which seats 250. The success was pivotal to their decision to acquire and renovate the Bagdad Theatre in 1991. (Photograph by Gary Lacher.)

The 1915 Kennedy School gymnasium on Northeast Thirty-third Avenue was converted in 1997 to another McMenamin brewpub theatre, seating 200, with 35 connected rooms for overnight lodging. Other local historic buildings now containing re-created movie screens include the 1911 Edgefield in Troutdale and the 1917 Grand Lodge in Forest Grove. Another, the 1905 St. Johns Dome, actually did present films at the Lewis and Clark Exposition that year. (Photograph by Gary Lacher.)

The Vanport Theatre was located in what is now Portland's West Delta Park. During World War II, this was a separate city—Oregon's second largest—built in 1943 to house and serve the many shipyard workers of the war effort. Besides complete city services, it had this 700-seat movie theatre. For several years, it ran 24 hours a day and changed pictures three times weekly. (Courtesy City of Portland Archives.)

After the war, population declined and urban decay set in. The famous Memorial Day Flood of 1948 destroyed the entire city and Vanport Theatre in a few short hours. All patrons escaped the theatre. This is the interior once floodwaters had receded and buildings were being stripped and torn down. (Photograph by Bill Hayes.)

Oregon's first drive-in theatre was just outside city boundaries, opening August 1946, sited inside the infield of Portland Speedway. That required speakers to be plugged into ground receptacles flush in the ground rather than on any dangerous posts. One mile from Vanport, the drive-in also suffered during the 1948 flood. It took a couple of months to get back in operation afterward. It closed in September 1980. (Courtesy Steve Stone.)

This is a 1948 view of the 800-car capacity 82nd Street Drive-In Theatre, which had just opened in March. This was the second drive-in for the Portland area but was the first with posts for the post speakers. The screen towers in this pre-CinemaScope era were the box type of enclosures. Closing in 1985, it was replaced by an indoor, six-screen cinema in 1987, which has in turn closed. (Courtesy OHS OrHi 22214.)

Several area drive-ins later sprouted additional screens, such as here at the 82nd Street Drive-In. Now the screen towers were designed much more like giant billboards, enabling wider screens. Of the nearly dozen area "ozoners," all are now gone. (Courtesy Scott Hicks.)

Oddly, this sign still graces the one-time site of the 104th Street Drive-In, which ran from 1960 until 1989. Now directing cars to a self-storage and warehouse facility, this sign is the very last local testament to a brief but common venue of movie exhibition. Oregon only has four drive-ins left, the closest at Newberg, about 20 miles from Portland. (Photograph by Steve Stone.)

Portland has always had film exchanges, necessary to distribute and care for film and related supplies. In the early years, they were scattered in the downtown area. In 1930, this much larger complex, the Star Film Exchange, was constructed on Northwest Nineteenth Avenue, between Kearney and Lovejoy Streets. Edmund Bidwell was the building's designer. The Star Film Exchange remained a busy affair well into the 1970s. (Photograph by Gary Lacher.)

Besides fireproof film vaults, there were offices for film studio representatives and two fully equipped trade screening rooms. This 1941 view is of one of many film inspectors, making sure prints were cleaned, repaired, or replaced before being sent out again. The complex also was home to businesses supplying equipment, concession supplies, posters, and theatre administration. These trades have all vanished, with space leased to other interests. (Courtesy Steve Stone.)

Portland could have looked much different, however. Over the years, many other picture house dreams, small and large, have been planned but not built. This is a 750-seat house, envisioned in late 1924 by the Golden State Theatre Company of California and designed by W. W. Lucius. It was announced it was to be located at Southeast Forty-first Avenue and Division Street, cost $125,000, and be a reinforced-concrete 150-by-100-foot building. (Courtesy Steve Stone.)

Another would have been the 1,500-seat Arabian Theatre, at Southeast Powell Boulevard where Foster Road branches off. The two-story, $250,000 structure was envisioned in 1926 by De Young and Roald, architects for the Sax Investment Company. Other significant theatres were announced for Northeast Killingsworth Street and Union Avenue, Southeast Thirty-ninth Avenue and Hawthorne Boulevard, Southeast Division Street and Fiftieth Avenue, and downtown on what is now the Pittock Block. (Courtesy Steve Stone.)

The Westgate Theatre in nearby Beaverton, Oregon, is pictured here on its final evening, November 20, 2005. The Westgate was a nearly identical twin to Portland's Eastgate Theatre on Southeast Eighty-second Avenue. Both led Portland and the state into the multiplex era. Both houses were upgraded as needed to stay flagships at the forefront. Both disappeared seemingly overnight, with little notice or thought. (Photograph by Mike Mathews.)

Westgate Theatre demolition is underway in April 2006, demonstrating how things have their own ways of becoming history before we are aware or even prepared for it. Obsolescence is making new chapters for future generations to reflect upon and research. The people of the Palace Theatre in 1908 probably saw and treated things in their day with the same casualness. History, and our participation in documenting it, marches on. (Photograph by Mike Mathews.)

INDEX

82nd Street Drive-In, 122, 123

104th Street Drive-In, 123

Academy, 116

Aladdin, 107

Alameda (30th Avenue), 94

Alberta (Victoria), 92, 93

Alder (People's, Music Box on Alder), 29, 30

Ames, 98

Amphitheatre Drive-In, 122

Avalon (Sunnyside), 100

Bagdad, 115, 116

Blue Mouse (Globe; on Eleventh Avenue), 72–74

Blue Mouse (Capitol; on Fourth Avenue), 83, 84

Bob White, 93

Broadway, 47–56

Brownie, 88

Burnside, 81

Casino, 81

Cinema 21 (State), 103

CineMagic (Plaza, Fine Arts), 101, 102

Circle, 82

Clinton Street (26th Avenue, Encore), 101

Colonial, 95

Columbia (Downtown, Century), 41, 42

Crest (Portsmouth), 90

Eastgate, 118, 119

Egyptian, 97

Elite, 89

Fox (Heilig, Rialto, Mayfair), 10–25

Granada, 96

Grand Avenue, 88

Guild (Taylor Street), 75–77

Hollywood, 109–114

Ideal (Senate, Crown, Elmo), 91

Irvington, 96

Kennedy School, 120

Kenton (Chaldean), 95

Laurelhurst, 104, 105

Liberty (Music Box), 45, 46

Mission, 120

Moreland, 108

Mount Tabor, 92

Music Box (at Yamhill), 78, 79

Oregon, 103

Oriental, 57–64

Orpheum (Empress, Hippodrome, New Pantages), 31–40

Pantages (at Alder), 31

Paris (3rd Avenue), 86

Playhouse (Baker, Dufwin, Music Box), 26

Portland (Paramount, Arlene Schnitzer), 65–70

Rio, 94

Roseway, 105

Round-Up, 84, 85

Roxy (National, Rivoli, Pix, Newsreel), 43, 44

Sellwood, 98

St. Johns (Venetian), 106

Star (Princess, 4-Star; on Fourth Avenue), 80

Star (in Sellwood), 89

Star Film Exchange, 124

United Artists (Majestic), 27, 28

Vanport, 121

Westgate, 126

Woodlawn, 90

ACROSS AMERICA, PEOPLE ARE DISCOVERING SOMETHING WONDERFUL. *THEIR HERITAGE.*

Arcadia Publishing is the leading local history publisher in the United States. With more than 5,000 titles in print and hundreds of new titles released every year, Arcadia has extensive specialized experience chronicling the history of communities and celebrating America's hidden stories, bringing to life the people, places, and events from the past. To discover the history of other communities across the nation, please visit:

www.arcadiapublishing.com

Customized search tools allow you to find regional history books about the town where you grew up, the cities where your friends and family live, the town where your parents met, or even that retirement spot you've been dreaming about.

MAP SEARCH